DESERT ISLAND WINE

by

Miles Lambert-Gócs

Miles Lambert-Gócs

Ambeli Press
Williamsburg, Virginia

Desert Island Wine

Published in the U.S. by:

Ambeli Press
1008 Settlement Drive
Williamsburg, VA 23188

Distributed by:
The Wine Appreciation Guild
360 Swift Avenue
South San Francisco, CA 94080
(650) 866-3020
www.wineappreciation.com

Library of Congress CIP Data:

Lambert-Gocs, Miles
Desert island wine / Miles Lambert-Gocs
p. cm.
ISBN: 978-1-934259-01-6 (1-934259-01-2)

1. Wine. 2. Humor. 3. Gastronomy.
TP548.L297 2007
641.2'2 – dc 22
2007021644

Printed in the United States of America

Excerpts have been reprinted by permission of the publishers and the Trustees of the Loeb Classical Library from the following works published by the Harvard University Press (Cambridge, MA):

Athenaeus: The Deipnosophists, Vol. II, LCL, 327, trans. G.B. Gulick, 1928

Athenaeus: The Deipnosophists, Vol. VII, LCL, 345, trans. G.B. Gulick, 1941

Columella: De Re Rustica, Vol. I, LCL, 361, trans. H.B. Ash, 1941

Hippocrates: Regimen, Vol. IV, LCL, 150, trans. W.H.S. Jones, 1931

Horace: Satires, LCL, 194, trans. H.R. Fairclough, 1926

Pausanias: Description of Greece, Vol. III, LCL, 272, trans. W.H.S. Jones, 1933

Pliny: Natural History, Vol. IV, LCL, 370, trans. H. Rackham, 1958

Plutarch: Moralia, Vol. VIII, LCL, 424, trans. P.A. Clement, H.B. Hoffleit, 1969

Theophrastus: Concerning Odours, Vol II, LCL, 79, trans. A.F. Hort, 1916

Xenophon: Memorabilia, Vol. IV, LCL, 168, trans. E.C. Marchant, O.J. Todd, 1923

The Loeb Classical Library is a registered trademark of the President and Fellows of Harvard College

IN MEMORY OF MY DEAR DAUGHTER,

VALERIE YANA LAMBERT

1978 – 2006

" *...twinkle little star...*"

"those who drink, after they have quenched their thirst, begin then to observe the ornamentation of the drinking-cups"

Plutarch

"the height of sagacity is to talk philosophy without seeming to do so, and in jesting to accomplish all that those in earnest could"

Plato

Table of Contents

1

LIVE FROM OLYMPUS

CNN ANNOUNCER: Good morning, viewers. We are ecstatic that CNN, after long negotiations, has been granted an historic, first-ever interview with Dionysus. Our crew reached the summit of Mt. Olympus at dawn, and we are expecting the Wine-god at any moment. As you can see, the place is a shambles. We can only imagine the ruckus the gods kicked up last night. However, they must be out and about creating havoc on Earth right now, because it's quite deserted up here. Wait a minute ... a figure is coming into view through the clouds ... I can make out a purple cloak ... and a heavy beard ... it must be Dionysus ... I say, Your Godship ...

DIONYSUS: Please, I don't stand on wine ratings, and titles don't interest me either. I am fond of sobriquets, though.

CNN: As you wish. We only know of your ways by hearsay, from ancient stories. We hope to learn more about your nature in your own words today.

DIONYSUS: Let us first take a seat over here on these rocks, and I will pour us a bowl of wine.

CNN: Oh, thank you. And let me also express our deep appreciation that you granted this interview. But as I look around I fear we may have come at an inconvenient time for your immortal colleagues.

DIONYSUS: You'll have to overlook the appearance of this place. There was quite a row last night over Zeus's latest flame, the mortal called Fergie. Zeus wants to invite her up and reveal his glory, or at least show her his tattoos, but some of the gods say she's too bawdy even for these halls.

CNN: We appreciate your candor. By the way, did you take a position?

DIONYSUS: Yes, I'll follow Zeus. Bawdiness is in my blood, as it were. I rather liked it when they used to call me 'oxhorn Dionysus' – a nice euphemism, that one.

CNN: Hmm, does that name explain why this wine tastes a bit rough?

DIONYSUS: Well, let me just say that elegance doesn't always go down smoothly with me.

CNN: Really? But what about Nectar? Among us mortals its name is practically synonymous with Great Wine.

DIONYSUS: I can assure you that your thirst for Nectar is misplaced. It's really only the full-blooded deities and the half-witted pundits who have any tolerance for such drinks. As you'll remember, I am human on my mother's side; I must suffer for it.

CNN: Do I detect a note of, shall we say, 'sour grapes'?

DIONYSUS: I have no reason to regret my human lineage, if that's what you mean. But my divine side can be a headache for mortals.

CNN: As our legends tell it, your mother, the mortal Semele, died before giving birth to you.

DIONYSUS: Yes, she was inadvertently vaporized by one of Father Zeus's thunderbolts.

CNN: And he rescued you and sewed you into his side and then brought you forth into the world himself, is that right?

DIONYSUS: You must be alluding to the Divine Gestation. It was like this: My father had big plans for me, but my olfactory organs had not had enough time to develop fully at the time of my mother's, er, accident. I could hardly have assumed my proper role without them, so Zeus did what he had to.

CNN: I should think, though, that you had a particularly close relationship with your father.

DIONYSUS: If you imagine that life with the old man was all *vin santo* and *biscotti*, you've got another think coming. He can be abusive – I mean, like when he zapped Mom and all. A fat lot of good Nectar ever did him. Besides, he was rather an absentee father. He gave me over to nymphs for them to raise me while he was out cavorting and spending my inheritance – the old boarding school gambit, you might say. But it was just as well for humankind, because otherwise you would have found me all spirit and no sense, and you wouldn't know wine from whiskey. 'Nurseling of fire' was one of my first epithets, you'll recall. That was before the nymphs wet me down and cooled me off.

CNN: Pardon my wondering, but it sounds as if your legendary prankishness might be a way of getting back at the world for your early suffering.

DIONYSUS: Prankishness? I don't know what you're talking about. I don't pull the wool – or this beard, either – over anybody's eyes. Everyone who knows me at all knows exactly who I am and how I behave. Here, let me refill your bowl.

CNN: I don't mind if you do. You'll be glad to know that I am finding this wine quite more to my taste than I thought at first.

DIONYSUS: Any honest-to-goodness wine will have that effect on any honest-to-Bacchus imbiber.

CNN: I'll remember that. You know, we were very surprised by your phone call and sudden reversal of position after having refused our requests for an interview so often in the past. We sensed some anxiety or urgency about it.

DIONYSUS: It's that Parker craze.

CNN: Parker?! He has caused a stir down below, but we had no idea he has had any impact on Olympus.

DIONYSUS: I don't take kindly to impersonators, and Parker pretends to speak with my authority.

CNN: You mean, he doesn't have your mandate? He certainly had many of us fooled into thinking he has the inside track with you. Why, just recently he claimed that you have some extra special wines you're keeping for him to score when his time comes.

Desert Island Wine

DIONYSUS: Well, he can expect this much: If he doesn't shape up, a greeting party of Harpies will be waiting for him when he arrives at the Styx. Just let him describe *their* bouquet. Can you believe that he had the chutzpah to fax me a subscription form for his newsletter?

CNN: I suppose he thought you might benefit from it. Many mortals would be at sea without it.

DIONYSUS: Now you understand my concern. People no longer have any faith in themselves where wine is concerned, which is to say they no longer trust in me. Just look at that numerical rating system. And to think that people used to call the Bacchantes mad.

CNN: But even you must pick and choose among wines, I'm sure.

DIONYSUS: Listen, when I went about spreading the vine my only thought wherever I went was to provide humankind with an elixir adapted to their place and to them. I am not the sort to go about anointing any particular wine. That business falls to my nemesis Hermes and his terrestrial troops of merchants and proselytizers. I frequently lock horns with that featherhead over labels and appellations and all his other gimmicks. I can get really fired up over it. In fact, let's just quench the whole matter with another bowl.

CNN: Indeed ... My! but this really is delicious. My guess is that it's from the south of France. Parker says you spend your summers there.

DIONYSUS: What did the French give him to say that? Give the French a few vines and the next thing you know they build a wall around them, call it a *domaine* and hire one of Hermes's henchmen to get them an inflated price. Is it really me they're honoring – or themselves? Sometimes I'm sorry I ever traveled over that way. Fact is, Hermes was offering a divine travel package I couldn't refuse. I was pretty gullible back then.

CNN: I didn't mean to make you so hot under the beard. But anyway, do tell me, what is this wine?

DIONYSUS: I call it 'bull's blood.'

CNN: Oh? The kind from Eger or the kind from Penedès?

Live From Olympus

DIONYSUS: Neither, it's just what I like to call it. I don't bother going out of my way for wine when I'm at home. I fetch this one right down below in the foothills of Olympus, in Thessaly. They tend a lot of cattle in Thessaly and my name has been yoked to bulls ever since people used to drink my vintages from oxhorns in the days before bowls. More bulls were sacrificed to me than you could shake a prod at. They even called me 'bull-shaped Dionysus.' I guess you could say the 'bull's blood' name is a sentimental favorite with me.

CNN: Does your sentiment also have something to do with what happened to your beloved satyr, Ampelos? He was killed riding a wild bull, wasn't he?

DIONYSUS: Yes, he was, and I did feel great sorrow about it, and even now the memory of it adds poignancy to my drink. But Father Zeus, who knew his plan for me, allowed me to keep my dear Ampelos in the form of the vine itself and to name it after him. Why, this very wine that we're drinking comes from the village of Ampelakia – a bittersweet bowl for me. As I've told you, regret is something I can never escape.

CNN: In light of all these associations with bulls, I must raise a question that bedevils some enophiles: Did you intend that all wine be red? There's your wine-dark beard, for one thing. I note, too, your purple cloak. And now there is this matter of the redhead, Fergie.

DIONYSUS: Sometimes you mortals are inscrutable. At one time, in the early days, I used to mix all colors of grapes together. Later, as I matured, I started separating them just to appreciate their individual hues the more, as though each were a rare stone. I never dreamed the tannin-tickled crowd would totter off into vinous bigotry. I'll tell you what the problem is: People don't spend enough time in the sun, my great ally – and that goes for your so called enologists, too. Anyway, if I had wanted all wine to be red, I'd have arranged it that way and Father Zeus would have backed me on it. But here, I think we need some more wine no matter the color. Say when.

CNN: To the brim will be fine ... So, speaking of the sun, where do you go to soak up some if not the south of France?

DIONYSUS: The past several years I've been going to Crete because a number of your wine writers have said it's far away from anything to do

11

with modern wine. Frankly, though, I've been disappointed in that respect. Cretan wine isn't what it used to be, and I can assure you that I remember the old days vividly.

CNN: Can we infer that you preferred the old days? And that reminds me – before this bull's blood gores my memory – the wine director at Christie's auction house has requested that we ask whether you might have stocks of pre-phylloxera Bordeaux that you would be willing to part with.

DIONYSUS: You might as well ask me for wine from the Trojan War. I live in the present time and I don't dip into relics. The styles of all ages have pleased me when they were right. I couldn't stand listening to those infernal Athenians prattle on about old wine at their symposia – and I have no patience for the decanter ceremonies of mincing Brits, either.

CNN: How far does your progressiveness extend, though? Would you ever consider, say, de-alcoholized wine?

DIONYSUS: I'll shave my beard before I have it.

CNN: I don't wish to be rude, but – now that you've bit the dog at the hair – there's been talk below that you have a drinking problem.

DIONYSUS: Some of these immortal blowhards up here have probably been whispering in the ears of the teetotalers and neo-prohibitionists down there. It happens from era to era. But what can I tell you? We gods are no more able to alter our nature than Aesop's animals can. That's how it is with the all-knowing and the dumb. Only you humans can change your ways. As concerns me personally, I am what I drink and I drink what I am, and I have no plans to enroll in a substance-abuse program in this lifetime.

CNN: I know our viewers will be very encouraged to hear that. Only don't be surprised if your next fax is from the U.S. Surgeon General.

DIONYSUS: Not a bearded one, I hope.

CNN: So, you really have no nostalgia for the wines of yore? But on the way up here I noticed an amphora of Chian wine in a cobwebbed crevice. And what about Naxos and its Bibline wine?

Live From Olympus

DIONYSUS: It was part of our agreement that we would not talk about Naxos.

CNN: We only agreed not to pry about your affair there with Ariadne, the Cretan princess. And I did not even bring her up when you mentioned Crete.

DIONYSUS: You make it sound so sordid, like this Fergie business. I did not imagine I was inviting tabloid journalists up here. Ariadne was different. She had a civilizing influence on me. What a shame she was taken from me so young. Who knows what I might have become? But Father Zeus knows best, I suppose. Ah, what sweet sorrow there is in my memories of Ariadne after a bowl or two.

CNN: I have no doubt about it. Parker says she was at least a '10.'

DIONYSUS: Are we back to that stuff and nonsense? Please don't bring out the worst in me. You know, when the Muses and I came up with the 'wine, women and song' theme we didn't have any 'hit parade' in mind. It kills the romance. Just ask Parker if he cares whether his wife is a '6' or a '5' by anyone else's standard. You ask me about that amphora of Chian wine. Well, I leave it where you saw it as a reminder that we lost Chios, and that it could happen to any other wine if my presumed devotees don't take equal care of all the wonderful sites I led them to. But come now, all this nostalgia could get depressing. I think you need some more wine to cheer me up. Or better yet, let's get up and dance the *hassapiko*, the butcher's dance. It's been a favorite of mine ever since the days of sacrifices. I'm a fun guy, you know.

CNN: I'm afraid you're going to have to help me up, Dionysus, old boy. This wine seems to have been too divine for me ... Viewers, our time with the Wine-god obviously is getting out of hand. So, we shall now switch you by satellite to our affiliate station in Baltimore, where a man claiming to be both the free-run Parker and the second pressing of Dionysus is in the studio demanding equal time. Adios from Olympus.

* * *

13

2

FIELD GUIDE

Name of Quarry: *Anthropos oenopotis* (Winebibber Man)

Description: Sometimes confused with *Homo sapiens*, *Anthropos oenopotis* usually can be distinguished visually by its more imposing snout and rump. Two body types occur: short, round and heavy, with soft epidermis, the so called Demijohn type; and big, long and weighty, with noticeable crustiness, the so called Jeroboam type. Advanced age is discernible from anthocyanin buildup in the extremities, not least of all in the snout and rump. Chemical analyses of fresh carcasses show remarkably low pH and high acid levels at any age.

Origin: Although little is known about the earliest days of the species, an origin subsequent to *Homo sapiens* is probable since *Anthropos oenopotis* would certainly have first put to its snout, not to its mouth, any fruit offered in the Garden of Eden, and likely as not would have rejected it on grounds of either under- or over-ripeness.

Early observers thought *Anthropos oenopotis* must have evolved from squatting beside campfires, because warmth gives rise to odors and encourages the making of aromatic distinctions ("If all things were to become smoke," noted Heraclitus, "the nostrils would distinguish them."). More recent researchers, however, cite the aromas of *grand cru* Burgundy, a long-time favorite of the species, and postulate that scatological memories might lie at the bottom of it all, whether or not *Anthropos oenopotis* would care to have its nose rubbed in the facts. In any case, its broadness of beam suggests that the species went to table ages ago and has hardly budged since.

Range and Locomotion: *Anthropos oenopotis* is widespread but avoids the torrid zone where corks steam and tops blow. Its preferred environment is the temperate zone, especially those *terroirs* which host other vine pests. But some individuals who are themselves feverish in disposition (possibly because of tannin deposits at nerve endings) are found at a remove from the vineyard belt; the scribbling members of the species typically are just beyond the fringe.

Movement for the most part is restricted to going to and from table, punctuated by scavenging treks to wine stockists. However, mass migrations to first-growth sites occur at spring budding and winter racking (see Breeding). When in motion, the nose is always held high and into the wind, with the result that *Anthropos oenopotis* sometimes faces the direction opposite to its forward motion, which has caused some observers to suspect that the species actually does not know Bacchus from its backside.

Habitat and Habits: *Anthropos oenopotis* is a cave dweller. Coolness and dryness are the minimal requirements sought for a cave; but elite breeds seek out tufa covered with the mold *cladosporium cellare*. The cave is situated away from noises and vibrations that might jar a precarious balance (in *Anthropos oenopotis* as well as in wine). Furnishings usually are of Limousin or Nevers oak. Sawdust of California redwood is spread over floor surfaces to absorb spillage, ullage and offending mouse urine.

In connection with the cave, the most notable trait of the species is its hoarding instinct. Wines are laid down so as to provide *Anthropos oenopotis* ample opportunities to give voice to its characteristic sounds (see Voice). It is estimated that each adult requires approximately ten cubic yards of bottle storage space per decade of its anticipated life span in order to remain suitably perfumed all the way to the end. However, the amount of space frequently exceeds this extent because of the congenital disposition to purchase and lay down wines for future enjoyment by favored offspring (recognized as those whose runny noses were wiped with hankies dipped in old wine and never sullied by detergents).

Semi-nocturnal in habit, *Anthropos oenopotis* is gregarious by nature and collects in gaggles that generally are convivial. However, fierce squabbles can erupt as to whether it is too early to broach a specific wine. Oftentimes calm can be restored only by mutual agreement to leave the wine in dispute to posterity, provided that it is certified as unfiltered.

Food: *Anthropos oenopotis* tends to crave high-fat and high-cholesterol foods, whether because of an intuitive faith in wine's counteragent role (*viz.*, The French Paradox), or simply because wine begets appetite (*e.g.*, 'on mange bien en France'). The tendency likely dates to prehistoric times, before the species had moved from the campfire into the cave; the atavistic attraction for smells of roast meat *in* wine has been cited as a proof.

Desert Island Wine

Dormice and deer on the spit reportedly are being replaced by eggplant and onion on the grill, but it remains to be seen whether the artery-clogging cheese addiction can be melted down. The species otherwise is extraordinarily fond of trace elements and dry extract content in its vittles, as in its drink.

Senses: *Anthropos oenopotis* depends largely on a keen sense of smell for orientation; however, the instinct can be skewed towards either a lofty pursuit of base smells or a base pursuit of lofty ones.

Some researchers hypothesize that the typical nostril-length fixation of the species may be related to a quest for aromatic lightness. This lightness refers to a swift but soft penetration of the nostrils by odors, up to the upper register of smell sensors located in the higher rhinal regions. According to this explanation, relatively long nostrils provide more time and space for the heavier vinous odors to fall by the wayside, until finally only the rarefied scents ascend. The seminal researcher Theophrastus noted that the species indeed strongly resists lesser smells and arranges the serving of wines accordingly ("certain wines if they are first drunk [allow] no satisfaction in others"). Even in the contemporary circumstances of greatly improved wine quality, *Anthropos oenopotis* continues to treat most wines as though they are only to be sniffed at.

Hearing is also thought to be a stimulus, and in some cases may actually substitute the function of smell. Thus, some individuals respond dramatically to distinguished place-names and varietal names but are unable to recognize plainly good wine if it is silently put under their nose.

Voice: The characteristic sound made by *Anthropos oenopotis* has been transcribed as BOO-KAY, which usually is sounded mellifluously following the swirling of tulip-shaped glasses. Also heard are a variety of nonsense ululations, sometimes throaty superlatives and sometimes high-pitched maledictions.

Breeding: Researchers are now convinced that mating in the species is determined along rhinal lines. Certainly no physical characteristic commands as much respect among members of the species as does a protruding proboscis; and rhinoplasty always has the contrary aim from the case of *Homo sapiens*, *i.e.*, nose jobs invariably are performed to add on cartilage and flesh so as to make, as it were, mounds out of molehills. The less well-endowed are usually observed skulking.

Field Guide

Particular significance is attached to the gathering known in the literature as the 'wine tasting,' which is presumed to be an elaborate mating ritual wherein a gaggle of *oenopotoi* assemble to flaunt prowess in maneuvering the fleshy facial organ to impressive effect and then make an expansive uttering. The behavior exhibited is thought to have strongly erotic overtones suggesting to the attendees just whom they might like to rub noses with. The advantage of image clearly is with the prominently beaked individuals in a gaggle, for considerable attention is paid to the noises they emit; the aberrant snub noses not infrequently become verbose, as if having to shout down the honkers.

The supreme form of the wine tasting is the 'blind tasting,' a sort of vinous guessing game in which the object is to discover the geographical, varietal and vintage origin of wines that are presented incognito to a gaggle. The greatest accolades are reserved for those individuals who are able to determine these origins just by the sense of smell, *i.e.*, without ever actually having to taste the wine. Thus are the men separated from the boys, and the women from the girls; and pairing and reproduction proceed. The high-nose-bridge British breeds are believed to have evolved to the sounds of adulation accorded over the generations at college-level blind tastings.

Both the male and the female of the species become sexually active during spring budding; but late frosts that prevent the spreading of blankets in the vineyards can delay coupling. Positions either in or beside first-growths are sought, usually downwind of the vats so as to engender multiple orgasm. Couples return to the breeding site for winter birthing, typically in a pomace clearing so that the newborn can be exposed immediately to wild yeasts. Kids with high olfactory thresholds are either abandoned or consigned to caddying wine paraphernalia.

Investigators have carefully collated data and report that population growth in the species is slower than in *Homo sapiens*, apparently because of reluctance to leave table. However, veritable population explosions take place as corks are anxiously being pulled in the range of 25 to 30 years after century-vintages have been claimed for the Médoc.

Tracks: *Anthropos oenopotis* leaves behind much recyclable detritus, increasingly including screw-caps, but never the plastic glasses gleefully employed by *Homo sapiens*.

Desert Island Wine

Accumulations of bottle labels are very characteristic. These labels, which perhaps serve as signals to wine condition, usually feature either a decaying *schloss* or a blooming flower; however, representations of naked body parts have been noted with some frequency in more recent deposits. Other printed litter is voluminous if repetitive, and typically includes photos, always in profile, of the elite Iberian breed, Domecqs. (Studies to determine a possible link between label *schloss*-es and Domecq schnozzles suggest libido arousal as a factor; but failure as yet to find depictions of naked body parts on labels recovered in the United States has left the matter up for grabs.)

Enemies: *Anthropos oenopotis* is set upon chiefly by purveyors of Burgundy and Gaja.

* * *

3

In probing the historical roots of residual wine hostility in the United States, some American enophiles have alleged that teetotal editors of the past, in fits of un-Americanism, pared away significant wine-related passages from American literary works lest readers uninitiated in the Dionysian mysteries be titillated to explore them. To parry charges of enophilian paranoia, I contacted hunters of first drafts to collect examples from various time periods, and herewith offer a trio of fearsome deletions concerning wine, from fictional American voices that were arbitrarily denied the Constitutional right to add …

THEIR TWO CENTS

MOBY DICK (Herman Melville, 1851)
Chapter 81, The Pequod Meets the Rose-Bud
Time Period: *circa* 1845

Captain Ahab enters his cabin with chief mate Starbuck after turning his back on the French whaler Rose-Bud (Bouton de Rose) because its captain had no information as to the whereabouts of the great white whale, Moby Dick. Ahab speaks:

"Tis warily that I gaze now into thy eye in these musty quarters and read in it the thirsty wish that I had boarded yon Rose-Bud, accepted draughts of claret, and set the Pequod on a commercial course. Aye and yes, that Frenchman's spout-hole expels none but claret, and claret is a mild drink for those owners of the Pequod whom thou art eternally prating about to me. Let those pudding-heads remain upon the lee shore and watch my sails billow with the body-less wind. Dost thou see in me a lubber? Sooner would I dissolve myself in crucibles of spermaceti than indulge bloodless claret upon this bottomless black sea. For mark ye, Starbuck, there is the blasphemy: to disdain the life-laden sea and pour claret's becalmed waters onto its troubling oil. Ahab is a nobler vintage, fed upon dry salted fare. Methinks my liquefied self would corrode the pewter into which they would pour me. Canst not thou readst in me the aching need for a grip in my wine – wine that can hold in this slippery world? This is not fathomed by those who defame me for spitting in the silver calabash. Aye, claret it was. Our Nantucketers would come about and sing of my verdict for all eternity as my topgallant deed if they but knew. Would that the calabash had been filled with Madeira, product of flames, much as though harvested from the try-pots of whaling men. Then would I have drunk deep and thrown no drop for earthworms. But thee, Starbuck, thou wouldst shun the accustomed Madeira of our fishing forefathers. Though a Nantucketer like myself, thou art of a sober and level-headed cast. Claret is thine. And I durst not touch claret.

"Yet claret is a mild, mild drink and has the unearthly calm of a mild sea beneath a smiling sky. Had I imbibed of claret a thousand lowerings ago, would Moby Dick have dismasted me? Had I perchance become a claret man, would I yet be on this heedless chase for the white whale, this chase that mordantly commandeers my soul's ship? Even more suited would I be to claret flavored with ambergris, as some of those merchants offer it, and to pour chalices of it through my gullet in the wake of ship-biscuit fried in blubber or whale steaks from the small as mate Stubb had black Fleece cook it. The whale's demonic essence in all its quieted unctuousness would flow into mine and this lashing torment of dark sea and pale spermaceti that rolls over me might end – or would never have been. For who knows when and where these things are written before they become. Aye, Madeira has stove in the lapstrake boat that is my brain. Oh, heaviness! Stout stuff is needed for woe to work on. But is it the Madeira, God, or I, Ahab, that fixes my lance on the white whale?"

*　　*　　*

THE RISE OF SILAS LAPHAM (William Dean Howells, 1885)
Chapter XII
Time Period: *circa* 1875

In the deleted original version of Chapter XII, the Vermont-born, Civil War-honed, self-made Boston baron of mineral paint, Colonel Silas Lapham, carries through on inviting the dilettante painter and Boston Brahmin, Bromfield Corey, to "a fish dinner at Taft's," and Corey accepts, as both men seek to take stock of each other's 'family values' in the gathering likelihood that Corey's son, Tom, who has joined Lapham's paint business, weds a Lapham daughter. The following conversation ensues at Taft's after they order their meal:

Their Two Cents

Corey purposed to elicit from Lapham a sign of assiduous urbanity and saw his opportunity in the wine card. "I hope you might care to share a bit of Sherry with me, Colonel Lapham. There is something so exhilarating about a Fino before oysters. I've always contended that it braces one for that plunge into the sea. I acquired this habit of mind so early that during my years in Italy I could not forbear ordering Fino even on the Amalfi coast. Of course it was not my intention to disregard the local vintages, although Italian dining companions may sometimes have been rather perplexed by my preference for Sherry over Lachryma Christi."

Without experience of Europe or wine, Colonel Lapham hoped to thwart this turn in the conversation. "I'm sure you've got the inside track on that, Mr. Corey. I hain't been accustomed to take any drink but water with my fish. O-o-o-h, maybe if there's tinned mackerel or sardines for tea I'll take Oolong with'em, but mostly I think water is about fit for fish. Wine must be kinda ha'sh on the fish, I should think, though I've noticed as how some of Taft's customers don't seem to swallow fish without wine. But, any rate, those ain't men of business. Pshaw! You're either cut out for business or you're not, and I'm not a-going to get myself mixed up with some harum-scarum supper customs."

Steadfastly focusing on the eventuality of a nuptial union between the two families, Corey probed for an opening towards a modest cultural renaissance for the Laphams. "I fancy that even if a glass of Fino would not suit you at the outset of your dinner, a man of your success should allow himself the enjoyment of a glass of Amontillado afterward. You might find the habit a boon to your business acumen. Depend upon it, the old families of Boston do not retain their wealth and status by eschewing wine, and anyone who thinks Mrs. Sayre has become a gifted humorist sought after for her company at Back Bay dinners by foreswearing Sherry and nursing Souchong is utterly mistaken. You might want to take advantage of next month's Library lecture on Sherry since your family is fond of attending such offerings. Don't forget, Colonel, you now have an agency in Cadiz, and if you find yourself there one day to learn about the mineral paint market in person, some knowledge of Sherry may stand you in good stead, because you will be in the neighborhood of the Sherry region and I can assure you that the local gentlemen, among whom you will find all the leading businessmen, will press Sherry on you."

Desert Island Wine

Sensing unshaped talents in himself and his family, Lapham was grazed by the nightmarish prospect that they were unsuitable culturally to preserve the fruits of his success into the future. He found himself groping for common ground with Corey. "Well, I just might jump at the chance to see a stereopticon about Sherry, as I hear that Cadiz and those parts are very sightly, but I don't know's I could digest a whole lecture on the subject. I knew an officer – a pretty good assortment, just in the mold of your Tom – who was in the 85th Massachusetts at Gettysburg, and I remember him talking on about Feeno and Uhmoantoledo by the campfire. I listened to him pretty much, figuring as how talking about it made him feel he was in a better place, and I couldn't blame him for that. But it was all pretty queer to me and I wan't able to follow him down all his byways. 'F course, if I'd been in mineral paint already I mighta caught his meaning about different grades of Sherry and the kinds they keep forever and a day, Reservies I believe he called'em. I don't mean to sit here in Taft's and go a-bragging up my paint to you over scrod, but fact is, ain't nothing leaves the factory as Lapham's Mineral Paint but what it was made with the genuine Vermont ore of seventy-five percent of the peroxide of iron and the very best quality boiled linseed oil. And as far forth as that goes, our fancy brand, the Persis – named for m'wife – don't have anything inferior to any wine that's been laying up in a barrel to improve on itself. The labels are A 1 too – the best that money'll buy."

Being foreign to the world of practical men, Corey had no comprehension of where Lapham might be headed with his allusion to mineral paint, and intentionally interposed an irrelevant mental picture that might serve to forestall a digression embarrassing to either himself or Lapham. "I don't know that I follow you quite, but I should very much like to show you a painting I did once of the interior of a Sherry winery, a bodega. I've never displayed it even at home because I made the mistake of producing it from a sketch while in Florence, where the light was rather mistier than along the Spanish coast and consequently influenced me towards a murkier rendering of the cellar than is to be seen in real life. But even so, you will readily grasp the general resemblance of the bodega to the arrangement of paint barrels in your storehouse and take away an affinity for Sherry that you perhaps cannot imagine now."

Lapham felt relief that Corey might be satisfied and the wine issue laid to rest by a social call to view a painting. "Phew! It's a good thing for me a man don't need much 'finnity when it comes to barrels of paint.

But I should think he *dooo* need a whole lot of 'finnity for spotting them differences between Feeno and Uhmoantoledo."

*　　*　　*

ROAST BEEF, MEDIUM (Edna Ferber, 1913)
  Chapter VIII, Catching Up With Christmas
  Time Period: *circa* 1905

After settling into her hotel room in Columbus, Ohio, traveling saleswoman Emma McChesney, of T.A. Buck Featherloom Petticoats, considers ordering her dinner from room service and recollects the recounting she gave to her Chicago friend, Mary, about a dining occasion in Columbus years earlier in her career in "one-night-stand country":

"Let me tell you, Mary Cutting, Columbus puts me too much at ease for my own good. And I don't think I will ever again be able to take my meals there without a side-dish of caution. And I'm downright queasy about hotel dining rooms in particular. I was gump enough one evening in Columbus on my first fall sales trip to accept the offer of a blamed wine salesman to share his table. But the dining room was filled to bursting with conventioneers and I was as hungry as could be from talking myself hoarse about featherlooms all day. Besides, I was new to the road and hadn't been put wise to Mr. Fred Seifert's brand of bunk. That was how he introduced himself, Mr. Fred Seifert of Sandusky, sole and exclusive representative of a winery somewhere by Lake Erie. He said he'd guessed from my equipage that I was probably on a small-town Midwest sales circuit. But he didn't waste much time on overtures and just went right into the first act. He took the extra glass on the table and poured me some Sparkling Catawba. I told him what I really wanted was coffee but he said it's a vile beverage for dinner and that dyspepsia was America's national malady because wine is ignored at mealtimes. Shucks! I was ingénue enough to swallow that, and the Sparkling Catawba too. But at the time I prided myself on being the modernest, the venturingest, and the copingest woman on the road, able to handle anything a man of my profession could dish out.

Desert Island Wine

"If only the women of Columbus didn't have the good sense to ignore the form-fitting skirt and stick to petticoats. I'd made a book's worth of sales that day and wanted to celebrate. I was going to order steak and French fried, but Mr. Seifert objected that the Catawba would be as out of place with the steak as truffles at a New England boiled dinner and that it would be a terrible thing to slight the Lake Erie perch at that season of the year. Perch season! My! How was I to know?! Not from the usual hotel food along my route. Besides, I'm hardly going to memorize every delicacy from Duluth to Cleveland. But Mr. Seifert said that that attitude was a tragic failing of Americans generally, and that if I got over it I would enjoy a great advantage with lady buyers along my route by being conversant with the viands on my sales territory. So, I shared a platter of Erie perch with him – and some French fried too, because I guess in all his years of wine-fussing he had not found anything against the Sparkling Catawba with French fried and all things thereto appertaining.

"I was ready to continue with the Catawba even after Mr. Seifert took the liberty of ordering creamed sweetbreads with mushrooms for us. But he had new glasses brought and filled with an Erie Sauterne, which he said is much praised by Americans in the know about wine. I liked it better than what goes by that name in New York, whether the kind from Upstate or the kind from France. It was really a pass between the two, without that bulge at the hips in the Upstate one or that frilly fringe on the French one. But what do you suppose Mr. Fred Seifert of Sandusky does next? Why, he sends in an order for pork chops. Breaded-and-fried pork chops. Germanic-to-the-core-Ohio-style pork chops. Ordinarily I'd probably have had hysterics, but Mr. Seifert assured me that the cook was a master and not a subscriber to the greasy and lardy. Anyhow, after that damage was done I was so forward as to express concern for my figure, but he said that any advocate of petticoats need hardly worry about the effect of an occasional pork chop or two. I told him that the only reason he could say that was because he hadn't seen me in a form-fitting skirt, to which he replied that seeing me in negligee would be more to his taste than even the Erie Sauterne. Lordy! if my petticoat wasn't climbing up about my knees by that time, Mary Cutting. That's why I always say a woman on the road had better avoid tickling the palate and just stick to tea and roast beef, medium."

*   *   *

The following article by a wine correspondent of questionable credentials was yanked from publication by a major wine journal lest it offend the core connoisseur readership by undermining their preconceptions.

4

COLONIAL FOOD FINGERED AS WHITE ZIN CULPRIT

At a press conference in Williamsburg, Virginia, an official delegation of California wine professionals announced that Early American food may be the root of all White Zin. As a result, the outlook for the ridiculed and embattled wine type is the rosiest it has been in years.

The California delegation had been dispatched to conduct intensive palatal-cultural research for the Memorial Agoston Haraszthy Select Commission on the Blush Plague after years of fruitlessly searching for hard facts by which to blame White Zin on American wine novices. The Commission expected to nail the matter down through Colonial agro-gastronomic documents and present-day consumer culinary depositions gathered outside bona fide wine country, and to conclude its work with a patriotic outpouring of anti-White Zin findings at Colonial Williamsburg.

The press conference was held at Chowning's Tavern following a groaning board luncheon orchestrated to lend weight to the remarks of the speakers. In his opening statement, delegation spokesperson Roger Grimfield, of the Association of Methuselah Zin Vines Estates, reported that the delegation's first inkling of the unexpected results came when White Zin proved to be "the hands down favorite" over red and white wines among sample Eastern Seaboard working class populations having verifiable Colonial-era ancestry. This included groups with such divergent ethnic origins and dietary habits as the lily-white watermen of Tidewater Virginia and the multi-hued melungeons of Appalachia.

Grimfield also reported that Colonial antecedents were found for 90 percent of the dishes being cooked at home in the coastal foothill regions of the Mid-Atlantic at the onset of the White Zin craze. He added that the research on food origins only occasionally led up a blind alley, as when jello molds could not be traced to an imputed salmagundi x syllabub cross. On these bases, the delegation's final report concluded that "the penchant for White Zin in all probability descends directly from 18th century burgher appetites and has no connection to the 20th century burger."

During its month-long labors, the delegation worked cheek by jowl with the Colonial Williamsburg Chefs of Revolutionary Cuisine in pairing a surfeit of retrograde dishes with representative samples of White Zin, Cab and Chard. White Zin received favorable scores in over two-thirds of the pairings, compared to a paltry one-quarter for Cab and less than one-tenth for Chard. The wine press assemblage reacted somberly to the data, but broke into sustained applause at the news that White Zin achieved its top scores with Smothered Dunghill Fowl among main courses, and among side dishes, Creamed Onions with Boiled Green Peanuts.

Delegation Lead Gourmet Debra Witherspoon offered explanations for White Zin's stellar performance. Her analysis led her to conclude, for instance, that Canvasback Duck with Pickled Barberries proved very satisfying only because "even the untrained palate might find in White Zin an echo – though pathetically distant – of Red Zin brambles." She also found that White Zin could only have bested its vinous brethren with Brunswick Stew because the free-range squirrel of the original recipe had been replaced by the close-quartered chicken of the neo-classical version. But Witherspoon's objectivity and credibility were compromised in the view of some attendees by her silence on White Zin's dunghill fowl triumph.

Speaking on behalf of delegation dissenters from the final report, Dwayne Lardmore, of the Central Valley's Vermillion Vineyards, expressed concern that White Zin enjoyed "a standing advantage" in the round-robin pairings because of its peculiar suitability with some recondite Colonial ingredients, such as the heirloom mealy How's potato. Lardmore further contended that "scoring was willy-nilly skewed in favor of White Zin by the ubiquitous presence of Sally Lunn bread and spoon bread with meals."

The Honorary Native American Palate for the tastings, Chief Clarence Brightcloud Ashe of the nearby Pamunkey tribe, likened the experience to "a long, long swamp hunt without the toasted marshmallows." But he emerged convinced that "White Zin is the best thing we've had from the White Man since beer in the time of my illustrious fellow tribeswoman, Pocohontas." He called the wine "a revelation" with Pamunkey weir-fished shad roe fried

Colonial Food Fingered as White Zin Culprit

in bacon fat, and said he was anxious to return to the reservation and try White Zin with gunnysack-trapped muskrat and his complimentary jars of pickled barberries.

A short presentation on the White Zin phenomenon was given by Marsha Gusti-Lerner, occupant of the Chair of Colonial Gastro-Anthropology at the College of William and Mary. Professor Gusti-Lerner emphasized that no statistical correlation had been found between White Zin preference and either low Intelligence Quotient or high Organoleptic Perception Threshold, as had once been predicted by the founders of the Haraszthy Select Commission. "To choose Chardonnay or Cabernet over White Zinfandel with either a Colonial relish tray or ham croquettes can only be justified by non-gastronomic guideposts, namely, by reference to what one's social betters have to say about it." Asked whether she thought Early American diners would have favored White Zin, Professor Gusti-Lerner replied, "Had White Zin been around then, it is unlikely that there would have been a Boston Tea Party."

*   *   *

5

REPORT TO TOM

It isn't easy, Tom, living here in the shadow of the nation's first enophile. I sense you looming when I pass your Memorial on the way to work and wine is on my mind. I would gladly entertain instruction from you, but you're more difficult to read on wine than on liberty.

Just the other day I could feel your glare again. You had wanted so badly for vines to be established as a branch of agriculture here in Virginia, and now that it's happening you see me still preoccupied with the exotic and devoting scant attention to the wines grown nearest to me. But you have to admit to being a xenophile yourself. Would you have replaced your Burgundy and Bordeaux purchases with Blue Ridge vintages? Pardon my saying so, but I suspect not.

Certainly the Virginia Wine Commission is not going to award me for my support of the industry. But I think I am doing as well as could be expected for someone who is not a native. I know wine drinkers with roots in this state going back to before the Revolution who have invested far less than I have in putting the Old Dominion on the wine map. During the 35 years I've resided here, which practically coincides with the life of the contemporary industry, I have sampled Virginia's wines whenever the occasion arose or your spirit moved me.

(My attitude has improved, too. I used to have a mental block about Virginia wine, like you had about hard liquor after your boozy freshman year episode at the College of William and Mary. I was in Newport News with the Navy in 1970 and one night drank too much of a sweetish purple wine from Virginia. It was named 'Sly Fox' and indeed it crept up on me and the next morning nearly made me seasick for the only time in my naval career. But 'Sly Fox' was made from native American kinds of grapes, and the contemporary industry has all but banished those.)

I must say, though – and please don't think Virginia is the only state I would say it about – that not everything about the industry sits well with me. Sometimes the wineries seem to be imposing their taste preferences on me according to their reckoning of the quickest route to acclaim and expect me to indulge them financially. Too often for my taste and pocket the result is a cosmopolitan price that does not deliver a palpably provincial flavor that I could ever feel nostalgic about. After all these years I still have no idea of what a genuine Blue Ridge expression of wine might be.

Wineries here usually come out of the starting gate with the driving ambition to be 'world class,' which results mostly in wines from prestigious internationalized kinds of grapes. Currently the producers are hell-bent on pinning their future glory on chardonnay. Recently I bought one for $20 (how's that for post-Louisiana Purchase inflation?!), whose claim on my wallet was that it was fermented with "native yeasts." I guess either my non-native blood did not rise to the occasion or the producers were defeating their nativist purpose by fermenting in French oak. My fancy is tickled most when the wines add something original on the subject of whatever the grape is. But that rarely happens. If Virginia can produce parochial quality regularly, it might prove to be from varietals or blends the industry does not think will earn it recognition outside the state soon enough. As you know, it takes time to find these things out. After all, you were experimenting with varieties of this and that vegetable for decades on end in your garden without reaching many definitive conclusions. But our wineries are born as if with all of their varietal conclusions already firmly in place.

The rush to institute Virginia appellations of origin has not elucidated much. It is symptomatic that all the appellation areas grow practically the same grape varieties. The missing flavors of place are merely being substituted by the appeal of historical place-names. I would not deprive you of the 'Monticello' appellation, of course. You deserve it, and besides, that has always been excellent country for fruit. But what is particular about 'Northern Neck' other than its name? Do you remember what used to be grown there? It was all tobacco in your youth and wheat in your maturity. Sure, you were happy about *that* switch, but why should we expect – or want – a Gironde on the Rappahannock?

It doesn't seem very wise at this point to have appellations that beg varietally precise definition. Given all the present circumstances, it might be enough for the time being just to have Tidewater, Piedmont and Shenandoah designations. These are the geographical divisions that every school child in the state learns, and they are probably as much as most adults can honestly hope to cope with in their glass as yet. We can leave some questions and details to later generations, the way you Founding Fathers did in the Constitution.

Desert Island Wine

Come to think of it, the wineries might do better to consult "we the people" a little more intimately if they want to come up with something specifically Virginian. And ordinary folks here might take more interest in the native wines if there were a grass roots aura about them. You must have had something like that in mind when you wrote to Sam Maverick in 1822 that wine should be a "domestic" branch of agriculture producing for family use rather than commercial sale. However, the days of the self-sufficient Virginia family farm you knew have long since passed, and families with no land for a vineyard except a lawn have to pay what they see as a high price for a bottle of decent Virginia wine. It's not going to convert as many contemporary Virginians to wine as you would like. I don't mean any disrespect, but let's face it, Tom, wine expenses contributed handsomely to your monumental indebtedness, and not many people are willing to wind up like you did financially because of wine. They'll sooner stick to iced tea.

(Frankly, Tom, I have to fault you on your pursuit of all the great names in European wine. Your connoisseurship would be a better example for us today if you had come back from your travels praising even one wine that had not already been lauded by the Europeans themselves. But you did not. It smacks of name-hunting. Even if I grant you the benefit of the doubt, it was a questionable legacy to leave to your impressionable countrymen. American enophiles are snickered at everywhere as being wine snobs in republican clothing. I wish you had been a little more – and I'm sorry to have to use this word – independent.)

I also think we would be better off if Virginia wines were being created with thoughts of Brunswick stew or chicken and dumplings or anything else that down-home Cavaliers have been known to cook when they are not subsisting on fast-food. But, as with the wines, the industry is more interested in following its own star in catering to foods. The impetus at the moment is behind Mediterranean ingredients and styles, although Virginia cannot grow the olive any better now than when you so disconsolately tried to cultivate it. But what kind of 'Virginia Wine' will that lead to? I do acknowledge, though, that chardonnay may be just the thing for that favorite dish of yours, chicken and mushroom *crêpes* with hollandaise sauce. Even I buy Virginia chardonnay – whatever the appellation of the yeasts – when the rockfish and *rémoulade* are running.

Report to Tom

I have wanted to ask you whether there is generally something 'sweet' about traditional Virginia dishes. Just remember all those native foods you missed while you were gourmandizing as our ambassador to France: sweet potatoes, corn, the peppers, the squashes, not to mention all the varieties of sweet peas you cultivated. American cooking habits in your day seem to have accentuated the natural sweetness of the indigenous foodstuffs. A cookbook of Colonial-era recipes that my daughter brought home from Williamsburg gives one for "baked spiced ham" that has a brown sugar glaze and reputedly was a favorite of yours (may Patrick Henry bite his tongue for impugning the patriotism of your palate). I also recall that you wanted to cultivate the Vermont maple for its syrup. Presumably, your household was also going to cook with the syrup, not just pour it over pancakes.

In any case, some Virginia chefs nowadays are bringing cosmopolitan techniques to the seasonal local foods. Recently at dinner in a hostelry in Williamsburg I ordered crusted catfish on a bed of rice with peanuts and corn kernels made crunchy through some artifice or other, and accompanied by sausage from Surry across the James River. The dish had a 'sweet' undertone and 'spicy' overtone, the latter from American red peppers like the ones you grew. The chef apparently thought he was creating a regional version of 'surf and turf,' although I trust you'll agree with me that squirrels and oysters would have been more like it. Anyway, I should have ordered a glass of the semi-dry riesling-vidal blend instead of the chardonnay.

Pairing native foods and local wines on-site is a challenge. I like roaming the back roads of the state in search of old regional dishes and always have hopes of finding good rustic wines on tap, like in a real wine country. But reality here is far from my daydreams. At lunch along the Rappahannock not too long ago I was disappointed that no Virginia wine was available except by the bottle; and I gladly would have let them charge me the usual exorbitant markup on a glass of local wine so I could have the psychic pleasure of quaffing something 'insular' with my soft-shell crabs and hushpuppies. I ended up with iced tea, like all the locals (free refills, too).

I have had to do most of my experimentation with Virginia foods and wines on my own at home. (Did you dabble in the kitchen, Tom? You seem like the kind of guy who might. And I presume that Sally's brother, the cook James Hemmings, might have given you some pointers.) Last fall and winter I was preoccupied with country ham and peanuts after reading that the hogs down in Surry and Isle of Wight used to be fattened on the remains of the peanut harvest. I came up with a *velouté* sauce for the ham using Virginia peanuts whipped to butter consistency. The dish would please you, I think, but most of the wines that accompany it well are off-dry whites and rosés, whether from European varietals or Euro-American hybrids. The only dry wine that impressed me with it was a red from a hybrid whose name I will not mention because our connoisseurs say it is not good for much. Maybe it was the salt of the meat or else the flavor of the unsalted peanuts that did the trick with that wine.

(I wish my head combined your nose for gastronomy and your faculty for taxonomy when it comes to combinations. But on second thought, did you fuss about combinations at all? We are told that you usually took your wine at the end of the meal, and that you not infrequently watered your wine. It's hardly even possible to speak of combinations in such cases. However, you obviously understood all about keeping your head clear around wine. And nothing could better demonstrate your grounding in classical Greek literature. I'll bet it was Athenaeus who clued you in, right?)

My daughter, who is a native Virginian, is enrolled at your old alma mater and brings home Colonial baked goods from the Williamsburg bakery. On her last visit she brought a currant-studded Queen's Cake. I opened a late-harvest Virginia vidal to sip with it, but it must have been from the wrong era of tastes. I found myself wishing I had bought a wine I passed up on one of my winery visits, a really odd dessert wine blended from Bordeaux varieties and native American grapes. The producer told me the idea for it came from a Colonial practice of 'sweetening' dry wines that arrived from Europe in a slightly acidulous condition. (Do you know anything about that? It sounds like something that might have appealed to George – Washington, not George III.) But I didn't buy any because it reminded me vaguely of that experience with 'Sly Fox' so many years ago.

At any rate, my daughter was horrified that I would drink anything but tea with the cake – obviously, she's a Tory as well as a native. That's one reason I always detour for wineries on our travels in the state: I hope she will eventually take an interest in the wines, which after all are her birthright. For now, she's attracted mostly by the design and décor of the wineries. But you, of all enophiles, can sympathize with her on that.

Report to Tom

Well, Tom, I apologize for taking so much of your eternity. You must have better things to do, like chiding the politicians who pass by here, and not just for their gastronomic indiscretions (don't worry, Tom, I won't go there). I hope, though, that this little *tête-à-tête* will prove as provocative for you as it has been therapeutic for me. You're a rational fellow, and you can trust me to tackle Virginia wines at my own pace. Just try to empathize with me a little more the next time I'm in sight. Let me suggest that it's the chardonnay clique and the iced tea crowd that you need to haunt. And, pardon me, but I think you have some explaining of your own to do.

* * *

All this is said by way of enologizing, or gulping down, as it were,
all the names of wines.

Athenaeus,
The Deipnosophists

6

APPELLATION PRAMNOS NON-CONTRÔLÉE

It confounds me how much flavor faith I can put in place-names. I found
myself doing it again at the farmer's market in Alexandria, Virginia, just this
week. It was the end of August and all of the produce stands were offering
cantaloupes and letting shoppers taste cubed samples. The sample at the stand
where I bought was very sweet and flavorful, but I knew from past experience
that this was not going to guarantee the qualities of the particular melon I
picked. No, what sold me was the sign announcing that these were 'Eastern
Shore' cantaloupes. It was the only geographic appellation posted among all the
melons being sold at the market, and you cannot live within striking distance of
the Chesapeake Bay as long as I have and not attribute quality to 'Eastern Shore'
when it comes to cantaloupes. Just don't ask me why.

I am in the same fix where wine is concerned. It was place-names
that drew me to wine in earnest to begin with, and I still make jaunts to wine
shops while hopefully murmuring geographic syllables as I go. It is as if my
palate will squeeze something extra from a mouthful when I can hang my
perceptions on the name of a region, village or hillside. Yet I usually have
no actual acquaintance with these places beyond their name and what others
have to say or write in their favor. But we have long been that way, we
enophiles. That is exactly how the ancient Greeks came to refer colloquially
to their most respected appellations by the term *xakoustos*, which signifies
'renowned' but literally means 'heard of.'

Our fascination with place-names can be traced as far back as
Pramnian, the ancient wine of the Aegean island of Icaria. Some Greeks
thought Dionysus was born on Icaria, but at any rate its chief settlement was
called, fittingly, Oenoi. The island's earliest vineyards were near a spot known

as the Pramnos Rock, and the Oenoians, by logic perfectly comprehensible to us today, began exporting their surplus wine as 'Pramnian.' It is the earliest known 'topographical site' designation used in wine trade. Such was the fame of Pramnian already by the time of Homer that he, well understanding his audience, as a matter of course dropped its name in *The Odyssey.* It would not have done for the sorceress Circe to offer Odysseus just any, no-name wine.

But we cannot be certain that Homer was thinking specifically of Icaria. For no sooner had Pramnian made its mark in Aegean wine trade than producers in other places began imitating it and marketing their replicas under its name. This began so early and continued so long that the length of time that names like Tokay, Port, Burgundy and Chablis have been misappropriated in recent centuries pales in comparison. Ten centuries after Homer, Athenaeus noted that the Pramnian name then referred only to a general type of wine, and that people had forgotten that it had ever been an indicator of geographic origin at all.

Questions may come to the mind of the 21st century enophile. Why didn't the Icarians take some steps to protect themselves from what seems to us the heinous commercial crime of wine fraud? Why didn't they devise a legal mechanism that would anticipate our systems of controlled appellations of origin? Consideration of such questions begs another one: Was there a fundamental difference in outlook between wine consumers today and those in the remote times when the Pramnian muddle arose?

Some historians of gastronomy have concluded from the ancient literary record that people then were generally more inclined than people today to link specific flavor with specific place, and therefore were also better at it. Certainly some of the ancients insisted on having food and drink of a particular origin, which is why the Roman writer Horace (*Satires*) was keenly aware of the self-deception to which his contemporaries were susceptible:

But what sense tells you whether this pike gasping here was
caught in the Tiber or in the sea, whether in the eddies between
the bridges or just at the mouth of the Tiber River?

Desert Island Wine

Concerning wine, the descriptive commentary of Athenaeus (*The Deipnosophists*) suggests that some ancient enophiles wanted guidance on flavor characteristics in confirming the origin of a wine as much as their modern counterparts do. What is even more condemning, the spread of the Pramnian name by imitation is strong evidence that not a few of the ancients were exactly where I am with Eastern Shore cantaloupes – they needed the reassurance of the name.

But way back in Homeric times wine drinkers generally may not have been concerned about wine fraud as we understand it now. In a more poetic age the co-opting of a place-name might have been regarded less a commercial ruse than a euphemistic suggestion of quality. From Athenaeus we know that even later on some people still had this perspective, since he related that the Pramnian name was applied "in general to all wine of good keeping qualities" (like ourselves, the ancients associated aging potential with wines from the 'heard of' places). By dint of practiced attentiveness to the perusal of colors, aromas and flavors, early Aegean wine customers could gain a sound general conception of quality, and honoring that fruit of the use of their senses, they might have considered it in the natural order of things that their conception of quality should be their first line of defense in assuring themselves the wine they wanted. Thus it would have been enough for them if a euphemism rang true to their senses. Such an outlook reflects an implicit belief that our senses, rather than the object we focus them on, must be the seminal point of sensory awareness.

And really, why shouldn't we be content to have good wine without fretting over its birthplace?

But our nature equips us with the capacity to respond to geographic and topographic appellations both rationally and irrationally. On the rational side, Hippocrates (*Regimen*) urged attention to origin as key to wholesome, beneficial consumption:

> …it is necessary to know the property, not only of foods themselves, whether of corn, drink or meat, but also of the country from which they come. So [for example] those who wish to give the body a stronger nourishment, without increasing the bulk of the food, must use corn, drink and meat from waterless regions. When they need lighter and moister nourishment, they must use things from well-watered regions.

Appellation Pramnos Non-Contrôlée

Hippocrates's analytical approach was based on his meticulous observations in the 5th century B.C. But the logic behind it must have originated in our primordial concern that food and drink not cause us harm. Just at the time that I was sampling Eastern Shore melons – at the very end of the 20th century A.D. – local fish-eaters were spurning the entire Chesapeake Bay catch in favor of Atlantic and Pacific appellations because of diseased fish that had been found in only three of the Bay's numerous tributaries. It was as if when the chips were down few fish aficionados were willing to bet that they could identify, in the fashion harpooned by Horace, which fish had gasped their last in the waters of the 'safe' names.

Once questions of health are out of the way, it may still be rational simply to want a repeat of a good flavor experience. When that happens we of course refer mentally to the places from where our previous experiences have come, the more so if we are interested in having a repeat of certain details of flavor. We must have picked up this habit of mind during our hunting-and-gathering days when we learned to return to the same 'hunting grounds' over and over again. We have a contemporary proof from my own neck of the woods, in the recent testimony of a Chesapeake Bay oysterman who stated that every spot for gathering oysters had its own name, and that for two-thirds of those spots "he'd tell you what rock [an oyster] come off of" just by looking at its color and shape. But his eye was an objective one in that he made his determinations only as a consequence of intimate familiarity, not out of a compulsion to declare one rock 'best' for oysters.

Irrationality comes into play when we go beyond these practical motivations and look to geographic origin to satisfy artificial psychic needs. A mild manifestation of this irrationality is when our hunger for place-names amounts to a 'paradise lost' nostalgia for the countryside, a vague longing to return to a time when we knew a name for every rise and rock and cranny of our immediate physical environment. This subliminal aspiration must date to the abandonment of hunting-and-gathering in favor of domesticity, since it develops after we have taken up residence away from the source of our food and drink. As our geographic distance from the place grows, we lose the solidity of harvesters like the Chesapeake oysterman. Instead, we cultivate a bent to attach mystical significance to geographic names that have lost concrete meaning and have become only seductive echoes. I am convinced, for instance, that part of the appeal to me of Eastern Shore melons stems from my childhood 50 miles upriver from the Bay proper in the nostalgically named 'Chesapeake Apartments.'

37

Desert Island Wine

More darkly, our irrationality can also take a turn towards egotistical self-flattery. Once we overhear our neighbors and understand that some place-names are more highly prized than others, we may begin expecting that certain names will not only be more pleasurable on the palate, but will also add to our own value. Athenaeus mentioned the case of the nobleman Demetrius who was brought before the court on charges of profligacy and thought to bring the reputation of the exalted Ariousian wine of Chios into the defense of his own:

> "But I am living as becomes a man of breeding as it is. For I have a mistress fair, I have never wronged any man, I drink Chian wine, and in all other respects I contrive to satisfy myself."

With our ego thus wrapped up in place-names, we feel resentment and indignation if we learn that we have been duped as to the origin of our wine. We will never admit, not even to ourselves, that we may have liked the wine just as much as if it had been what it was purported to be. No, we want the head of the merchant-perpetrator. Unable any longer to see the mischievous smile of Dionysus, is it any wonder if true enjoyment of wine also becomes a casualty of our irrational reverence for place-names?

Today's appellation of origin mechanisms are in part a response to the irrational concerns that lead to the breakdown of our sensory involvement. Viewed from that perspective, regulated appellations represent a subconscious last resort to protect ourselves from the mistakes into which our own nature as impressionable consumers can lead us. Paradoxically, appellations may also be the straw that breaks our backs as appreciators of wine.

The concept of controlled appellations is not a recent one. The germ of it appeared quite early, again suggesting the ancients' similarity to ourselves as enophiles. In the 5th century B.C. (just when Hippocrates was expounding on the rational virtue of ascertaining origin), the wine traders of another Aegean island, Thasos, took measures, including the stamping of amphorae, to legally affirm the origin of their highly reputed wine. But this was already too late for Pramnian. Icaria had been enslaved a century earlier, thereby receding as a wine exporter and losing its stake in the Pramnian name.

Appellation Pramnos Non-Contrôlée

The Icarians in any case would not be blameworthy for what we might regard as commercial neglectfulness. Even though concepts related to appellation systems would crop up autonomously now and again in later wine history, the idea of the Thasians did not catch on and last. It would not be until the 20th century A.D. that we systematically and consistently set about ordering and extending measures for the protection of geographic names in wine.

We have not yet finished elaborating our appellation control mechanisms, and debate goes on even now as to just what they should be expected to accomplish as far as their impact on consumers is concerned. Some people hope that through careful formulation and application of the appellation systems wine drinkers will develop a surer feel for the connection between region and flavor. And that is alright with me, because it is no more, really, than what I should hope to achieve in the case of Eastern Shore melons.

But there are more optimistic hopes, if optimistic can be the word for it. Some observers of the appellation scene look for the control mechanisms to ensure not merely typicity of regional characteristics but also guaranteed gradations of high quality. It is in effect to look to taking assessment out of the hands of the person who is drinking the wine. It is a notion, I daresay, that was inconceivable when Icaria began exporting Pramnian.

*   *   *

7

EARTH SCIENCE 101

The only real regret I have about my undergraduate studies is the mediocre effort I put into Earth Science. And I was already showing signs of becoming a serious wine lover, too. But I had eased into wine labels directly from stamp collecting and therefore looked upon wine only as another pursuit subsumed under geography, even if one that offered a more tangible taste of places than philatelic artwork could. I had yet to read any of the wines-of-the-world books and learn that wine appreciation is more specifically a branch of geological inquiry: schist, gneiss, sand, gravel – all can leave their sensory trails in wine. I would have taken Earth Science more seriously had I known. Instead I have had to try to make up the course-work on my own over the past three decades. As a result, I have come up with a course of study for other *amateurs*:

THEORY

Geo-enology is an ancient area of inquiry. In fact one of the oldest of wine terms is the Greek *geodes*, or 'earthy.' But the concept of wine as a reflection of earth is not any the less confounding for its antiquity. On the contrary, wine's relationship to the land it grows on still brings our gustative vocabulary to its knees.

The Ancient Era

In early times the smells of earth must generally have been presumed good. We have proof from Athenaeus (*The Deipnosophists*): "Do you note how sweet the earth smells and the steam is coming forth with greater fragrance? It would seem that some seller of frankincense dwells in the chasm, or else a Sicilian cook."

The Greek term *aroma*, which in wine appreciation eventually replaced the earlier term *euosmia* ('good-smell'), appears originally to have come about from the smell arising from the earth itself while it was being broken for cultivation, since *arotron* was the Greek word for the plough and *aroura* the word for ploughed land. Plutarch (*Table-talk*) even related that Dionysus was regarded as the original ploughman.

The 4th century B.C. naturalist Theophrastus dealt with geo-enology systematically. In *De Causis Plantarum* he examined the properties of vines, as well as the flavor properties of their fruit, in relation to soil, water, temperature, wind and other aspects of the physical environment where vines are grown. He identified the entirety of these factors by the term *chora*, or 'country' in the multi-dimensional sense of land-space: "Since not only the varieties of vine but also the *chora*s differ, we must endeavour to distinguish what varieties are appropriate to what *chora*s."

In another of his works, *Concerning Odours*, Theophrastus provided an explanation for soil's occasional precedence among the various environmental factors when he observed that earth is "the only elementary substance which has a smell." In conjunction with his concept of the *chora*, this insight implied that the smell of land is not only general, but can also be specific to the specific locale or site, the *topos*.

Plato, in the *Timaeus*, indicated that water was the carrier of earth as it courses through the vine. That is, water becomes suffused with traces of soil that can leave their mark behind in plant tissue and fruit. Thus, the 1st century A.D. Roman agriculturalist Columella, in *De Re Rustica*, recommended hands-on advice to avid soil investigators of his day:

> ...from that part of the field which displeases us most, clods should be
> dug and soaked in an earthen vessel, then thoroughly mixed with
> freshwater and, after carefully straining in the manner of dreggy wine,
> examined by tasting; for what is the taste transmitted by the clods to
> the water, such we shall take to be the taste of the soil.

The significance of 'dirty' water to wine appreciation can be inferred from Athenaeus, whose discussion of water points to the lumpy kind as the likely origin of applying the term *geodes* to wine.

Since Columella focused on taste in the strict sense, namely on mouthfeel sensations, his instruction also demonstrated the general disrepute into which the term 'earthy' had already fallen as a flavor description: poor quality land had become associated with questionable flavor, and vice-versa.

But Theophrastus (*Concerning Odours*) had been careful to distinguish mouthfeel from aromatic flavor, and suggested that atypical tactile sensations can be by-flavors of sound origin that are inseparably linked to favorable aromatic sensations:

> To speak generally then…things which are least of an earthy nature have a good odour…But, even as many things pleasant to the taste present a certain bitterness, so many things that have a good odour have a kind of heavy scent.

The Modern Era

In a passage reminiscent of Columella's ancient advice, Mark Twain in 1883 noted that when Mississippi valley people find "an inch of mud" in their water glass they don't hesitate to stir it up and "take the draught as they would gruel" (*Life on the Mississippi*). But the Mississippi folk clearly were out of the mainstream. The overall trend in modern times has been toward increasing ambivalence about the gustative pleasures of soil. Indeed, water, our essential liquid, by and large has not been tasted as a means of geological discovery for some time. This is apparent as early as the 19th century, when the gastronome Brillat-Savarin (*The Physiology of Taste*) asserted that "water has no taste." So, too, the direct impact that soil can have in healthy vinous flavor usually is not acknowledged by today's enophiles. Just the opposite, in recent years there has been a conscious downplaying of the role of land, as such, in the concept of *terroir* (which is the successor term to the *chora* of Theophrastus).

In modern wine literature, geo-enology has received attention mostly in connection with the French tasting term *goût de terroir*, or 'taste of the land.' In 1816, in *Topographie de Tous Les Vignobles Connus*, André Jullien defined *goût de terroir* as a flavor "communicated to the wine by the ground [*terrain*] on which it was harvested." However, the term is deficient in that it cannot convey from one person to another exactly what taste is to be conjured. In his 1950 book, *La Dégustation*, Norbert Got frankly sized up *goût de terroir* as "an indefinable sensation resulting from diverse impressions."

Goût de terroir's vagueness as a flavor description has not deterred us from using it as a qualitative indicator. In that function, we have in practice almost always given it pejorative connotations. Jullien, for instance, left a favorable impression of a *goût de terroir* only once in the several specific cases in which he mentioned it as being characteristic of the wine of the places concerned. More recently, a decade-long flap occurred over California wines, with the French criticizing certain of them for displaying a *goût de terroir*, while the Americans came to the defense of the accused in a ground swell of native-soil sentiment.

Goût de terroir has also lent itself to widespread confusion. By at least the 19th century people were no longer reacting to a flavor that might be indicated by the term, but rather to the term itself. Thus, upon noticing a sensation that might justify the term, the imbiber recoiled in the certainty that it must be a negative quality. In 1801, the scientist Jean Chaptal, in his *Traitée Sur La Culture De La Vigne*, emphasized the frequent misapplication of the term, especially the tendency to call any disliked savor a *goût de terroir*. For instance, in 1812, the gourmand Grimod de la Reynière quoted from an earlier letter in which the expression was used in decrying the ersatz 'Champagne' then flowing in Poland.

Chaptal distinguished "natural" from "artificial" occurrences of a *goût de terroir*. Natural occurrences, he said, were "inherent in the nature of the soil and independent of the will and work of men" and were more often favorable than not (fetid smells and unrelieved bitterness being examples of unfavorable though possibly natural instances). In contrast, artificial instances were incidental either to vine cultivation (such as over-manuring) or to wine making (such as lumps of earth getting into the fermentation vats); and Chaptal considered these occurrences always a "vice." Edouard Feret, in his 1898 dictionary for wine professionals, echoed Chaptal in noting that either grape growers or wine makers can influence the occurrence of a *goût de terroir*, and explicitly stated that the expression can be used positively as well as negatively.

But it fell to Got in 1950 to recover for modern enophiles the insight of Theophrastus. Got made the organoleptic distinction that a *goût de terroir* may manifest itself in aromatic as well as mouthfeel sensations. He was inclined to consider aromatic manifestations as natural occurrences, and mouthfeel sensations, which are more strictly earthy (*terreux*), as being of suspicious origin. Got was even more positive than Feret about most cases of a natural *goût de terroir* because of "agreeable odorous substances having their mark [*cachet*] of origin." It has everything to do with distinctiveness, that indispensable impression without which even high complexity has clay feet.

PRACTICE

Earth usually is not directly a part of our gustatory experience, or at least not once we step out of toddler-hood into a cognitive frame of mind. Geo-enology, consequently, is the sort of terrain where we can easily lose our sensory footing. Field work is of the essence.

Laboratory #1 – *Goût de Terroir*: Narrow Sense

Coming across earth in the smell of wine is not as common as it may sound. It is found in vivid relief, however, on the island of Santorini, an extraordinary lump of earth-stuff in the southern Aegean Sea, whose traditionally made ('rustic') wines do not permit of convincing replication elsewhere.

The vinous spelunker is wont to account for the unique Santorini flavors by resorting to images of the weird *topos*. For instance, early Western travelers let the island's volcanically mutilated landscape suggest to them, in misleading simplicity, a sulfurous aftertaste. However, Santorini's ashen overlay of earth, lack of moisture and perennially drying winds may be extremely favorable to earthiness of flavor. In the Theophrastean cosmos, earthiness shares some origin with bitterness, and thus tends to be augmented by loss of moisture.

By purposeful use of their ancestral wine making procedures, home wine makers on Santorini routinely dig up vinous truffles – and without occasioning inroads on wine health. Notably, they employ partial dehydration of grapes to a greater or lesser degree for all their wines, from white through red and dry through sweet. Also, wood has no chance of covering over earth in flavor since the traditional maturation practice is to use well maintained old barrels. Not everyone, however, may care for the resultant flavors. For example, the *Larousse Dictionnaire Universel de XIX*

Siècle was critical of a *goût de terroir* in Santorini wines which "displeases in France." But as Chaptal pointed out, the term had already become a cultural sand trap for the French by that time. The earthier Russians could not get their fill of Santorini wine.

Laboratory #2 – *Goût de Terroir*: Broad Sense

A *goût de terroir* can shift under the weight of the recently expanded comprehension of the term as an amorphous taste stemming from the entire micro-environment. The North Fork of Long Island – a distinct *terroir* but one without true grit – is a case in point.

The North Fork is a new viticultural landscape that has no fixed flavor image as yet. The local wine growers are still feeling their way about the terrain. Chaptal emphasized that even on the same land an occurrence of a *goût de terroir* might be favorable or not depending on the type of vine; and a full roster of esteemed grape varieties is being cultivated on the North Fork. But it remains unclear which ones offer palpable flavor features that can be chalked up to the natural conditions, and which ones do not. As earth loses ground to the other environmental factors subsumed under *terroir*, those varieties which actually impart traces of the turf may be eliminated by growers who have no taste for it – or who sense that their customers do not.

In order to isolate gustatory sensations that derive from the land itself, perceptions of North Fork wines might be checked against the gamut of vegetables and fruits that are also grown in the *terroir*. After all, analogous sensory features might be detectable. The observations of Theophrastus would suggest that the relatively more bitter vegetables generally have the advantage in such a comparison. Nevertheless, the most direct path to identification of Earth's topical gustatory markings might be through the cucumber, water's true interlocutor in the vegetable world.

SELF-STUDY QUESTIONS

Are austere wines more likely than sweet wines to leave the taster between a rock and a hard place as regards *goût de terroir*?

Desert Island Wine

Are dehydration of fruit and evaporation in wine more favorable to flavor outcroppings of soil, sub-soil or bedrock?

Is earthiness most perceptible in initial taste or aftertaste? Or, does it hold the middle ground?

Does new oak hinder perception of earthiness in wine? Would earthen vessels enhance it (in other words, ashes to ashes and dust to dust)?

Does perception of earthiness grow with age? the wine's? the taster's?

Is all stemware equally effective in presenting earthiness? Does cut crystal have any advantage? stone goblets? clay cups?

Can earthy flavors be surmised from vinous color? (for instance, are taupe highlights a giveaway in new white wines? sienna in new reds?)

Does our contemporary broad definition of *goût de terroir* in effect invert Got's description of it in its original, narrow sense? That is, has his formulation of 'an indefinable sensation resulting from diverse impressions' now become 'an indefinable impression resulting from diverse sensations'?

Will Jullien and Chaptal roll over in the ground if they can hear us standing them on their head?

*   *   *

8

THE TERROIR TERRORIST TALKS

The first thing you notice about the house from the outside is that no windows face the landward side of the property. This might not be remarkable for an old New England family that made its fortune in the Colonial sea trade, but the owner happens to be a disinherited scion who built his own fortune by grappling with land – or more narrowly, *terroir* – for six decades. Now he has literally turned his back on the firmament and passes many hours watching the Atlantic Ocean and musing about the earnestness, credulity and yearnings of his former customers.

We are along the Cape Cod coast, at the home of William 'Billy Buds' Granville, the most notorious peddler of phony appellation wines since Cassius Aurelius of Pompeii. He quit the business ten years ago, and with the statute of limitations now safely behind him, he feels he owes humble wine lovers an apologia laying out his rationale.

But don't imagine that Granville feels remorse or contriteness about his chosen line of work. "It's not as though I took people's money without giving them what they wanted. If they wanted a sniff of Romanée-Conti, I gave it to them with all the trimmings, and at fair prices. Where else were they going to get that? And without my price-rectifying influence, the wine market would have crashed a dozen times during my career. Go and tell that to the wine wonks who whisper about me in dark cellar nooks."

It cannot be overstated how badly Billy Buds feels about being treated as a pariah by the wine press corps. "On the one hand, you've got a cadre of MWs who are scrambling their taste buds to identify every known wine blind. And on the other hand, you've got the scorecard hacks who basically know what they're tasting and take it apart using the wine aroma wheel. So, of course they're going to resent somebody who's instinctively got appellation savors down pat and can ideate them so as to take wines D, H, J and M and create a ringer for wine Q. It's strictly a case of palate envy."

Desert Island Wine

Granville is anxious to put to rest speculation that he gained his inimitable skills through nose-to-the-dregs apprenticeships in Europe. He points out that he needed no formal training at all and never left New England until he was 47. His grandfather's cellar had been richly stocked since the mid-19th century with wines brought from Europe in Granville bottoms. "It was all child's play to me. Cap'n Gramps Granville spotted me as a wine prodigy by the time I was six. He's the one who started calling me Billy Buds." By that time, the future master wine forger could already distinguish *grand cru* Burgundy from first-growth Bordeaux even in 40- and 50-year-old bottles.

But his early prowess did not necessarily destine Billy Buds for the nefarious side of appellation regulations. That path was taken instead because of an emotionally charged home life with demanding parents who wanted him to squelch his palate and "do something useful" with his life. "But what was I going to do?" Granville asks rhetorically. "Take over my father's CPA practice? I suppose it would have helped me become a conventional wine pundit, but I was beyond that tripe by third-grade."

After high school, young William was expelled from the family home and not provided with a stipend. This brought him face to face with what he regards as the central reality of being an enophile: "The hallowed wine names do not deliver on their price." But it was only after a day spent slogging through hundreds of wines at an exhibition that he saw the light. "I had never tasted so many wines all at one time, and after the Italian pavilion I realized I could take five or ten or sixteen unheralded DOC wines and make them into esteemed French AOC wines that sell for more than any of the components but still less than the originals. It was downhill coasting financially after that."

At first Granville was only interested in self-gratification ("What else is so called wine appreciation about?"). But then he found that he could win enophiles and influence markets by going commercial. His company, GranVin, was soon offering an array of prestigious wine names at prices below the competition – and earning high marks from wine reviewers. If anything, it was the consistency with which GranVin aced the score sheets that raised some eyebrows in trade and journalist circles about authenticity. As one befuddled and begrudging competitor put it in one instance, "No Graves tastes that gravely Graves." But Granville is quick to deflate the chatter of his critics: "Even leaving their sensory deficiencies aside, it would have taken more palate honesty about the presumed lesser wines than the average wines-man could muster."

Consumer conditions did not remain static during Granville's career as an appellation thief. He says his biggest challenge was in staying on top of trends and fads. "Nobody can get fixated on some one thing so fast and furiously – and then drop it just as suddenly – as wine people do," he explains. "And you have got to deliver on whatever that thing is that they're currently looking for, whether it's 'Old Vines' or 'Organic' or what have you. The trick is to tweak your wine so as to meet the customers' preconception about the word and win over their impressionability." Besides, Granville found himself mentally stimulated by changes in enophile focus. "It prevented my mind from stagnating. Mindset freeze is the most common ailment of both the garden-variety enophile and the elysian pundits."

Asked about the 'reign of *terroir* terror' at the end of the millennium, the man whom the French government decried as 'the *terroir* terrorist' gives a response bound to shatter enophiles who came of age in that era: "*Terroir* made my work too easy. Any diversion from appellation 'true' could be touted as *terroir* 'true,' and it would be swallowed like mother's milk by the *pauvres petits*. Now, *that* was a field day for a charlatan with no appreciation of the pathos of the ardent enophile. Given the temptation, it was really a strain to remain an ethical wine forger."

But did an appellation ever get the best of Billy Buds? Was he ever stymied in creating his facsimiles? "There were several *terroirs* that exercised me. I was never quite satisfied with my Colares, for instance, although nobody else knew any better. But now we're talking about hard-core, inimitable *terroirs*, the macho *terroirs*. And take my word for it, there are far fewer of them than enophiles like to pretend there are."

Our host disappears momentarily and returns with a bottle labeled Colares. "I like to sip this and watch the Atlantic of an afternoon. I didn't pay enough attention to tides. I wasn't a real Granville, and my Colares wasn't quite 'on' because of it." But we wonder aloud whether it's the real Colares we're drinking. His unabashed response sums up his philosophy, his career, his life: "What would be the difference? It's what's wanted."

*　　*　　*

The following are excerpts from a taped conversation between the author (MLG) and the owner of Gobs-of-Fruit Vineyards, Brad Crostati. Any similarity between Mr. Crostati's statements and remarks made in the popular press by other American wine producers is purely non-fictional.

9

VINEYARD WITH A VIEW

......

MLG: I couldn't imagine writing about directions in American wine without talking to you, Brad. So many wine folks consider you an architect of the future.

CROSTATI: Thanks. Well, you know, when you're making wine it's not enough to be contemplating your micro-environment in real time; you've also got to have a big picture.

MLG: How do you see things? What is your worldview, so to speak?

CROSTATI: Everything we're doing here starts from the premise that we've got Yesterday, Today and Tomorrow wineries in this country. Wanda [Mrs. Crostati] and I certainly want ours to be ahead of the curve: Wherever American wine has got to go, we're determined that Gobs-of-Fruit will get there first.

MLG: How does that translate for you in practice? I presume you're referring to technology.

CROSTATI: Not as such, not anymore. Technology per se was good enough for the 1970s and 80s, but if there's one thing we learned during the 90s, it was that technology can bog you down. Like, if you insist on sticking to a specific fermentation temperature vintage in vintage out, it's going to limit your stylistic maneuvering. It's time for American wine to move on to the next stage in its development, and those kinds of obsessions won't get us there.

MLG: Where do you expect the changes to come?

Vineyard With a View

CROSTATI: Most of them are going to be in the vineyard. In fact, that will practically define the next stage. I'm not saying we've answered all the questions in the cellar; but out in the vineyard we haven't even raised all the questions. Right now, too many wineries are Today indoors but Yesterday outdoors. American wine is only going to advance when we've completely stopped letting *terroir* play second fiddle to technology.

MLG: What are you looking at here at Gobs-of-Fruit?

CROSTATI: Mostly plant density and leaf cover. We've got to stop bending *terroir* to the extrinsic molds imposed by technology. But you can't hope to know your *terroir* if you're not growing your fruit optimally. I don't want to sound apocalyptic or anything, but if we don't tackle issues like spacing and canopy head on and soon, the Aussies are going to have us for dinner – and I don't mean our wines.

......

MLG: Can you tell me about your locale here and how you chose it?

CROSTATI: Our inspiration was Shifting Sands State Park, the topographical emblem of the area. Wanda and I were raised out here and feel strongly that this defining feature of our ecosystem should impact our wines. You have to honor the life essence of the land even if that means putting its demands ahead of the larger appellation district. And being natives, we feel we've got the inside track as to what that should mean in terms of style and flavor. It's the thing that really gets our juices going.

MLG: Shifting Sands? I'm not familiar with it.

CROSTATI: This is Pliocene territory, and when the northerly winds blow they drive sandy particles from the opposite shore and deposit them over here. Along the shore on this side you can find long mounds of sand that accumulate as high as 10 feet and submerge the tree trunks. There's nothing else like it in the appellation. It makes cluster hang time a tricky proposition.

MLG: Sounds like it could be ruinous for your vines and fruit.

Desert Island Wine

CROSTATI: Believe me, Wanda and I chose this site with utmost care and we try to use the environment itself for extra protection. We've got the right elevation, and a stand of trees lower down near the shore catches a lot of the sand. But we also take other precautions. You'll notice that the vine leafage is left heaviest towards the north. Plus, the winds blow strongest outside the growing season; so, during the growing season we put up fine nylon mesh barriers on the north-facing sides. The mesh catches large particles that could strike the clusters laterally and lethally at high velocity.

MLG: Hmm, you're describing a kind of a pre-filtering of the terroir, aren't you?

CROSTATI: Fortunately, you can't hold back *terroir* so easily. Sand blows in over the barriers. It's just that then it merely drops in vertically, by gravity, and does not hurt the fruit, especially if the canopy is right within the parameters of the hang time. But still, we remove two tons of sand a year from our vineyards each fall. It's definitely worth it, though. In the short run we get better ripening of the grapes from the reflection off the sand; while in the long run we have some insurance against phylloxera. We're even considering an experimental plot of ungrafted rootstocks.

......

CROSTATI: We had an MW from England here recently who much preferred our barrel-fermented version and said he could even mistake it for a Chassagne-Montrachet. Hearing things like that puffs you up a bit momentarily, but deep down I don't think a Tomorrow winery in this country should want its chardonnay mentioned in the same breath as a renowned white Burgundy – even in a favorable way – because otherwise what's the point of taking the pains we do? And it really makes you wonder about the role of ML.

MLG: Actually, it makes me wonder more about the role of MW. But what do you mean, Brad?

CROSTATI: Just that malo-lactic fermentation might be inimical to an expression of the Shifting Sands *terroir* in our chardonnay.

MLG: So, no more ML?

CROSTATI: I don't think we'll stop using it entirely. Some people simply like ML because of the buttery-ness, and that's a market we can't afford to ignore in the present stage. On top of that, we've noticed that we get better structure to support the *terroir* flavors in our white Meritage, especially in mid-palate, when we keep it a few months on the lees from our ML chards.

MLG: Does clonal selection figure much in getting what you want from chard?

CROSTATI: We're always looking into the clonal angle for all our grape varieties. Eventually we'll be working from quite an extensive database relating to clones and clusters. Our priority in the case of chard is simply to distance ourselves from tropical fruit flavors, no matter whether we ferment to dryness or not. Tropical fruit may be okay for Yesterday or even Today wineries, but not for us, not on our mission. We don't want full-blown flavors at Gobs-of-Fruit anymore. We believe in moderation and want as much finesse as we can get. That's where the clonal/cluster database is going to be a big help – as soon as we understand exactly what the data are saying.

MLG: Last year's steel-fermented chardonnay had an unusual facet and I'm supposing that's the sort of thing you mean.

CROSTATI: Right. A lot of customers commented about that, and some told us it reminded them of the delicately sweet corn they buy from farm stands around here. We like hearing it too, because our micro-environment practically dictates that nuance. It's not good enough just to be true to the appellation. You've got to be specific to the vineyard, to the vines right in front of you. That chard is grown on a parcel we purchased from our neighbors, the Rutkowskis, who used to grow corn on it and still own the fields surrounding it on three sides, where they still grow corn. We can't prove it absolutely, but we think the corn influences the wine somehow and can be regarded a 'secondary' *terroir* factor even though it's not intrinsic to the landscape. In fact, next year we're going to label our steel-fermented version 'Rutkowski Fields Chardonnay.'

......

MLG: It sounds like you don't filter.

Desert Island Wine

CROSTATI: We have a healthy skepticism about filtering. Because when you're passing wine through the mesh you are in a sense tampering with the *terroir*, and Wanda and I are sensitive about that because of our deep attachment to Shifting Sands. But since it isn't clear in all respects what the next stage will entail, we are constantly experimenting with filtering as well as fining. Wanda feels the only crucial thing is that, whatever we do, we keep the cola nuance in our cabernet. This seems strongly characteristic of our *terroir* where cab is concerned, and we don't want Gobs-of-Fruit to lose its identity among all the other cabs on wine store shelves.

MLG: But how do you know prior to fermentation that you're going to get the cola? Do you resort to a Brix reading or seasonal weather data?

CROSTATI: We've pretty much abandoned the Brix obsession in determining ripeness here at Gobs-of-Fruit, and instead we just sink our teeth into the grapes out in the vineyard. If the grapes don't taste right out there, forget it. We want fruit that rings true to Shifting Sands while still carrying a varietal tune. You simply don't find that out from Brix. Brix belonged to the 70s and 80s. The future belongs to canopy and spacing.

MLG: Apparently you're pretty satisfied with your wine making.

CROSTATI: We're not home free yet. We've got to work on tannin – everything from oak chips to polymerization. After all, you've got to turn a rough tannic bite into a soft kiss to the extent your *terroir* allows it. We've discovered that we can achieve that with our cab and still get the cola nuance if we gently irrigate the cap during fermentation. Punching down the cap can turn the cola to coffee; and that's just not going to be anywhere in the next stage of U.S. wine evolution.

MLG: I take it that becoming a Tomorrow winery doesn't mean switching from cabernet.

CROSTATI: It's not likely for the life of the current plantings. But to demonstrate the change in our thinking, we have a great new site that I once would have considered worthy only of cabernet. I'd have put in a Bordeaux blend like cabernet sauvignon, cabernet franc and petit verdot. But instead, we're putting in ramisco from Portugal because of its affinity for sand. Of course, no wine from it will be really ready to drink for a decade, but we're banking on being on the cusp of the next stage by then, and that's also when root ball growth should start kicking in qualitatively.

......

MLG: You must have a pretty comfortable rapport with your customers, since they so willingly move along with you from one 'stage' to the next.

CROSTATI: We try to, but it can be tough. Most of them are tourists, drive-bys from the city. Nearly 300 cars pass by daily, mostly because of Shifting Sands, and in the summer it's close to 800. But our only chance to rub elbows with any of these folks is in the tasting room, and after a while you get to the point where you only want to deal with people who understand what you're doing. Otherwise, why bother? But if a wine still doesn't sell, we get the message and won't be able to stick with the concept over the long haul no matter how much we believe in it. That's why customer education is so critical if American wine is to reach its potential.

MLG: How about the local people? Have they taken to the winery?

CROSTATI: It depends on just who you're talking about. Lately we've been getting some gentrification out here, with a lot of GenX-ers moving in from the city. We're very pro-active towards them and try to bring them in for special events like our Fourth of July Grilled Veggie Fête and the Labor Day Alternative Music Concert. The Baby Boomers are no longer driving wine sales, and in any case their frame of reference simply is not where a Tomorrow winery is going to have to be.

MLG: Actually, I was thinking more of the families that are rooted here.

CROSTATI: Unfortunately, except for the Rutkowskis, who buy a few cases of our steel-fermented chard every year, the old-time families have not been very interested in what we're doing. We're trying to give them a stake in our success by getting the local restaurants to work with them on supplying their kitchens with produce – you know, a 'local food and wine' thing. I've even stopped saying 'my' wine when I talk to them, and say 'our' wine instead, so they'll at least start identifying with the appellation zone overall. Then maybe we'll be able to convince some of them – or at least the ones with compatible micro-environments – to grow grapes for us. It would help our economies of scale, which is especially important now that gentrification is driving up land values. That's a downside to the GenX-ers.

MLG: How do finances play into your decision-making?

Desert Island Wine

CROSTATI: Finances have imposed some stylistic constraints in the past. We're going to have to escape that in order to move forward. We're getting into agricultural diversification and have already undertaken a number of projects. Some of these could give us a head-start in the switch from organic to biodynamic that we see on the horizon. Right now our vineyards are only organic on the verge of biodynamic. But Wanda is already doing biodynamic gardening and selling produce, plus the Crostati family pasta sauce, at a stand of our own along the main road to Shifting Sands.

MLG: *A Tomorrow winery is sounding a bit like a Yesterday farm.*

CROSTATI: 'Lifestyle' is a byword for Wanda and me. But while we don't favor a 'big ag' approach, you've got to be flexible in this business. We've got to ensure a short-term cash flow while we're incurring the added costs of pressing ahead. There's no other way to make it through to the next stage.

MLG: *Any other plans for that, Brad?*

CROSTATI: We'll have to play it by ear. But Wanda says we ought to change our name soon. She thinks 'Gobs-of-Fruit' is too Today.

......

*   *   *

10

ON A FINER POINT OF WINE

Having observed the tendency for viewers of his dance arrangements to become distracted and less appreciative if they were made privy to how the pieces had been designed, the choreographer George Ballanchine was reluctant to discuss the framework and details of his compositions. He would have understood implicitly the unfavorable effects on wine appreciation and assessment that can be wreaked in the name of wine quality by some wine commentators who will not cork it on points of wine technology beyond the ken of laypersons.

*

Providing information about technical wine production methods has long been a part of popular wine literature. We can find such information as far back as Pliny the Elder. We might even suppose it a reasonable pursuit, provided that it is accomplished without adversely affecting the reader or appreciator. But since the late 19th century, as enology has steadily advanced, the task of providing information on wine making techniques has entailed ever more effort, and has drawn non-enologist wine buffs ever further into the province of enologists, even though few of the amateurs have any thirst for actually cracking the enological tomes.

A growing inclination of some wine writers, who tend to forget that at best they are no more than the cream of the buffs, is to be not merely carriers or reporters of enological information, such as it comes to them, but also partisan critics of wine technology. We might spy a touch of that proneness in the first works of modern wine writing in the early 19th century, although it was restricted to unusual techniques and found fault only in the case of methods whose failings were established in the first instance by the inferior, usually diseased wine that resulted. But ever since H. Warner Allen criticized pasteurization in his 1932 book, *The Romance of Wine*, some writers have also taken to passing judgment broadly on techniques that develop out of science rather than custom, even when much more has remained to be learned of actual effects and possible control of them – and without much considering the wine itself.

Desert Island Wine

The notable instance that crops up with some frequency in the popular press today is filtration. Typically, the technique is censured as being anathema to 'fine wine.' Starting out from a semi-mystical notion of 'natural wine' as that to which nothing is added and from which nothing is taken away, filtered wines are called 'eviscerated' and 'emaciated' or even 'lobotomized.' We are told further that a would-be producer of 'fine wine' would resort to filtration only for the expedient, compromising, mercenary purpose of being able to offer the wine for sale sooner, and for earlier drinking, thereby speeding up turnover of wine stocks. The facile, seemingly common sense arguments and vivid language of the anti-filtration writers are so compelling that the reader is liable to take the opinion of the writers for enological fact. Yet, the facts presented by enologists in their writings demonstrate that, at least on this heady technical subject, 'common sense' does not stand up to reason.

Filtration is the process by which wine is pumped through mesh pads which adsorb, or attach by attractive power, and sieve, or hold back by physical blockage of passage, colloidal and mucilaginous material (including such material that remains after racking, which is the transferal of wine from one cask to another in the course of barrel maturation so as to leave behind impurities that have settled out as lees). The process may vary in the material from which the filter pads are made (typically asbestos or cellulose), the porosity of the pads, and the number of passages to which the wine is submitted. The choices made depend on the purpose of the filtration, which must reflect the nature of the wine and its qualitative potential, as well as its condition (the point in the wine's maturation at which it is to be filtered). A special case is 'sterile filtration,' employed at the time of bottling, which consists of passing an already very clear wine through densely packed cellulose fibers to remove remaining colloids. (Anti-filtrationists usually appose filtration to fining and leave the impression that fining, which is the dropping of agents, such as egg whites, fish glue, bentonite, etc., through a wine to gather up and remove suspended material, is the 'natural' and therefore conscientious choice to 'clean up' a wine. But enologists point out that the two procedures are complementary rather than inter-changeable.)

Since filtration as it is practiced today was developed in the 20th century, it has been subject to extensive examination and monitoring by enologists throughout its development. Writing in 1937, the Hungarian enologist Sándor Pettenkoffer advised, "we should guard against exaggerated

On a Finer Point of Wine

filtration [of quality wine], repeated filterings not being to the wine's advantage." The French enologist Jean Ribéreau-Gayon, writing in 1947, indicated that even a single filtering can put "very good, bouqueted *vins fins*" at risk if the filtration is "extreme" relative to what the wine requires. The decision as to what will be extreme requires objective information about the wine, because, in the more recent words of the enologist Émile Peynaud (1984), "it is observed in practice that different wines do not behave in the same way in relation to the same filter surface." Jean-Claude Berrouet (1986), a prominent Bordeaux enologist, says, in reference to the *grands vins* of that region, that "certain wines ought to be filtered and that some others can have it dispensed with." Ribéreau-Gayon effectively summed up empirical findings such as these with the caution, "a general rule [regarding the effects on 'fine wine'] cannot be formulated."

Some anti-filtration writers can unfurl intimidating scrolls listing names of reputed wine producers who support their contentions, and who indeed would not knowingly touch filtered wine with ten-foot stemware. Enologists have been all too aware of this stratum of anti-filtration sentiment. J. Ribéreau-Gayon (1982) remarked on "the resistance of certain professionals" who regard filtration, especially sterile filtration, "almost a necessary evil" that thins wines, even though "numerous verifications prove the reverse." He also noted that because of their views these persons use less dense filtering plates if they decide to employ filtration.

Peynaud points out that since filtration is strictly a mechanical procedure it *cannot* be inherently damaging to a wine. Events incidental to the filtration, however, can have a negative influence on the result. Ribéreau-Gayon (1947) emphasized that, when evaluating a filtered wine that differs in smell or taste from its unfiltered sample, it is necessary to distinguish between effects due to the passage of the wine through the pores (the filtration per se), and "the effects which are owing to secondary phenomena." The secondary phenomenon most often mentioned by enologists is oxygenation: "Often one attributes to filtration effects which owe, in reality, to the aeration" brought on by the necessary pumpings that push the wine through the filters, which may contain a significant amount of air (Ribéreau-Gayon, *et al*, 1982).

Some producers who resist filtration have perhaps experimented with it and hastily read their preconceptions into initially displeasing but possibly transitory results:

Desert Island Wine

> [In certain cases] after filtering, the wine loses some little part of its alcohol, aromatic material and carbonic gas content and will be tired; however, this drawback occurs rather just in open [to oxygen] filtration and such a loss is not completely avoidable in racking either, besides which the carbonic gas and other material is replaced after a short time and the wine regains its earlier freshness. (Pettenkoffer, 1937)

Filtration can also be wrongly planned or executed. Notably, sterile filtration – so evocatively terrifying in sound – must be conducted in a sterile environment, using equipment specially designed for the task. The procedure requires expense and skill, and some producers who are not up to one or the other would sooner point the finger at the process than at themselves. Peynaud (1980) wrote that when performed correctly a filtration does not thin wine, but rather will improve it by removing "internal stains." He further pointed out that to argue the opposite is tantamount to saying that "the quality of wines is due above all to some suspended substances which are foreign to them!"

Certainly the subject of filtration would ordinarily have no more appeal for the lover of wine than dry cleaning has for the lover of finery. But filtration has found fertile soil today, when the consumer, facing a bewildering assortment of goods, often hopes to latch onto a piece of information by which to ensure beforehand that the quality sought for will be there after the purchase. One of the handles we might reach for – no matter our capacity to deal with it – is production technology. We simply collect information on how the product was made, and then compare the findings to the mental list of *do's and don'ts* that we have accumulated, possibly without requisite care and from questionable sources.

The problem confronting the taster in comparing filtered and unfiltered wines is that of singling out the presumed influence of filtration from effects which might in fact be owing to some other aspect of a wine's coming into being. Yet, anti-filtration writers usually suggest that any enophile worth his or her lees will be able to spot a filtered wine anytime. Their blandishments in that vein can persuade impressionable readers to put knowledge of a wine's processing ahead of its tasting, as when we are out shopping for wine and reflexively reach for the bottle featuring – virtually as

On a Finer Point of Wine

though an appellation name – the word UNFILTERED. For amateurs, this is a backward approach to wine, inimical alike to spontaneous appreciation and conscientious assessment. For as Peynaud (1980) put it, having "the preconceived idea that filtering tires and weakens wines" will cause even an otherwise fair-minded taster to perceive the most limpid wine as "less fat and more stripped [of its substance] than the other."

The trap of self-delusion frequently involves the propensity to dredge up words to support a preconceived conclusion. Impressionistic, definitionally 'soft' words can be used to highlight relatively stronger or weaker qualitative aspects of the respective wines, and thereby justify the prejudices of the person tasting. For instance, an unfiltered wine that has actually suffered a loss of quality over time, possibly because of something endemic in its 'wholesomeness' that has come back in its older age to haunt it, might be graced with a phrase like 'added complexity.' The antidote to the opportunistic use of words is to keep in mind that wines of comparable quality may not have the same quality advantages: "Wines can merit the same [qualitative] mention with very different qualifiers" (Peynaud, 1980).

Tastings that enologists have conducted in accordance with strict scientific procedure, under laboratory conditions (not those of, for instance, a producer's cellar), have demonstrated that, at least in the case of 'fine wines' which should have been filtered, and which have been filtered in a way tailored to them, the filtration is not detectable. Ribéreau-Gayon (1982) went so far as to say that "if all the precautions are taken" there is rarely a perceptible difference between the filtered and unfiltered wine during formal organoleptic inspection: "The filtration in itself does not affect the quality of the wine."

*

For all its modernity, the filtration controversy has ancient roots. In the 1st century B.C., Horace (*Satires*), ever with tongue in cheek, ribbed pretentious Roman gastronomes of his day with a formulation that he knew certain of them, not suspecting his intent, would fully endorse, since it was just the sort of thing they themselves might spout while under a head of steam:

Desert Island Wine

If you set Massic wine beneath a cloudless sky, all its coarseness
will be toned down by the night air, and the scent, unfriendly to the
nerves, will pass off; but the same wine, when strained through linen,
is spoiled, losing its full flavour.

More than a century after Horace, in the late 1st century A.D., a
debate on filtration was recorded by Plutarch in his *Table-talk* (VI. 7, 692-
693): "Question 7 – Whether it is right to strain wine." The guest Niger,
noting that early Greeks had called wine 'lees' because they conceived
of its essence as residing therein, argued that to remove from wine that
which "constitutes the edge and power" is to "cut [it] off from its root,"
and thereby render the wine lesser in quality. One even finds in Niger's
arguments the sort of metaphors and moralistic intonements that issue from
anti-filtrationists today:

"This practice reflects a tendency to over-refinement, vainglory,
and luxury, and sacrifices the useful in favour of the pleasurable.
To castrate pigs and cocks, making their flesh unnaturally soft
and effeminate, is typical of men whose health and character are
ruined by gluttony. Just so, if I may use the metaphor, do people
caponize and emasculate wine, filtering it because they are too poor
in health to drink hard and too intemperate to drink in moderation."

Aristion countered that filtration amounts to "no more than a cleansing away
of corrosion and dirt," much as with the processing of wheat into bread, or
any other sort of removal of "sediment or refuse." As to Niger's broader
charges of finickiness, Aristion answered, "You might speak of everything
we have here as overelaboration, beginning with the house."

*

Sometimes I remember that wine is supposed to be all about
civilization and rationality, and wish that the anti-filtrationists would stop
dropping crummy Suggestion in our ear. But at other times, as when I am
overcome by the superiority of 'stone-ground' loaves over baguettes (those
eviscerated sticks) or of so called 'dirty' (skin on) potato chips over the
kind made for the queasy, I feel that the anti-filtrationists do not go nearly
far enough. At those times I get to thinking, for instance, of what was the

most remarkable wine I ever tasted – a wine that made the word OINOS pop involuntarily into my head. Grown below the Parnassus of the ancients, that wine was not only unfiltered but also was made from the fruit of sixty-year-old vines that never saw phylloxera or American root stocks. Surely it was this last circumstance that accounts for the extra something that made that wine so strikingly, so quintessentially, winy. I could even think, in that frame of mind, that we might just as well forego all post-phylloxera wines, including the unfiltered ones, and go back to water, remembering that Plato (*Timaeus*) identified wine as a form of water "filtered through the plants of earth."

* * *

11

CONUNDRUM

"Solid tastiness." It certainly does sound inviting. Something to sink your teeth into. We might sooner say it in unqualified praise of a ripe peach, but in this instance the phrase has been lifted from wine literature, where its use can be less straightforward.

Solid tastiness. Hmmm ... a monolith of flavor? It sounds like a deficiency of complexity, if you ask me. But there are wines, little known ones, say Račianska Frankovka from Slovakia, in whose case a spade may be called a spade, and others, widely esteemed ones, say St. Émilion, in whose case a cryptic formulation like 'solid tastiness' must be devised to save face both for the wine and the appreciative imbiber describing it. Not that there is any necessary shame if one's wine is insufficiently perplexing in aromatic profile. It's just that these days we have taken to basking in the radiance of brooding Complexity, in whose cavernous chapel we have erected a graven image to Bacchus.

Let's not leave the wrong impression about the age of our fascination with complexity. Even the ancient Greeks were onto its scent. From the 5th century B.C. we have the evidence of a poem by Hermippus, in which he elatedly praised an aged wine for smelling at once of violet, rose and hyacinth. A century later, Theophrastus (*Concerning Odours*) explicitly differentiated 'simple' from 'composite' smells and clearly anticipated us in his reaction to the latter:

> ...the more numerous and the more various the perfumes that are mixed, the more distinguished and the more grateful will be the scent...[In] perfumes of this class the aim and object is not to make the mixture smell of some one particular thing, but to produce a general scent derived from them all.

The term *symplektos*, literally 'knit together,' also had sensory connotations to the ancient Greeks, and indeed it is this term that has come down to us through the Latin as 'complex.'

Conundrum

But no talk about complexity intruded on the pages of wine literature of the modern era through the 19th century. Wine writers then did not even set out descriptions like that of Hermippus. One of the groundbreakers was from outside the gastronomic field altogether, Lewis Carroll, whose description in 1865 of the bottled marked 'DRINK ME' in *Alice's Adventures in Wonderland* was of prescient significance for enophiles of the late 20th century: "a sort of mixed flavour of cherry tart, custard, pine-apple, roast turkey, toffee and hot buttered toast." (Carroll did not identify that beverage further, but I have it on the authority of a more fortunate wine drinker than myself that it could only have been Tokay Essence 1811.)

It seems that the age of Freud was needed before complexity could be addressed as such. At any rate, it was not until 1932 that the term got its initial boost in English-language wine literature, in H. Warner Allen's *The Romance of Wine*. Allen made reference to complexity by name several times while discussing how grapes ought to be processed so as to maximize the multiplicity of "nuances." His mentions of complexity were only peripheral, though. Allen did not actually broach the topic of complexity as a sensory notion. As a result, he bequeathed us a word without parameters, but one with plenty of room for spontaneous interpretation and arbitrary application, which is no way for the accumulation of wine vocabulary to proceed.

A particularly hazardous implication of Allen's legacy is that complexity should be construed from the perspective of wine making procedures. The temptation to do so might come from our experience in the kitchen, where the immediacy of our involvement first as the cook and then as the consumer of the food we eat persuades us to attribute complexity to something we have been conscious of doing during the preparation:

It could be as simple as fettucine with olive oil, garlic and
tomatoes to which fresh arugula is added at the last minute
and tossed until wilted, or a more intricate medley [such as]
fusilli tossed with dandelion leaves, arugula, watercress,
fennel, tomato, garlic, and hot peppers.

However, to come to a verdict on complexity in wine by an analogous route requires both thorough knowledge of the arcane aspects of wine chemistry as it flows from wine making, and the equanimity that can be – it

65

is not always – fostered by the technical knowledge, in order that imagination is banished while we are considering how a particular wine was made. A layperson approaching complexity from the technical side despite a lack of technical training is liable to draw cause-and-effect relationships that have no basis in fact, and that therefore are bound to influence erroneously the assessment of a wine:

> "The case in which we say the false opinion arises: when a man knows both and sees both (or has some other perception of them), but fails to hold the two imprints each under its proper perception; like a bad archer he shoots beside the mark and misses it; and it is just this which is called error or deception."

(Socrates, in Plato's *The Theaetetus*)

Any wine enthusiast who wants to determine complexity will find the task sufficiently complicated even when it is confined to what can be made of a wine while we have it in the glass. We are especially prone to get a foot caught in one or another bight in the line when we drop our sensory lead line through a wine's 'layers of flavor' to ascertain its 'depth.'

The misstep that repeatedly pulls us over the side is our tendency to take any sensation as a true perception. But a sensation only becomes a perception when it is relatively stable and can be stowed in our memory for some period of time after the sensory experience itself, so that we have 'on file' a sort of mental picture to which we might return. Yet perception is subject to fluctuation, and our conscientiousness in reporting on what we perceive is threatened anytime we take soundings at the outer shelf of sensation. This is the borderland where Brillat-Savarin's "fleeting nuances" are at play: "students of them assume…a proper stance for the pronouncement of their verdicts, always with necks stretched and noses twisted up and to the left, as it were to larboard" (*The Physiology of Taste*).

Nuances present the situation in which imagination is tempted to speak out in our identifications and judgments. But a 'perception' that arises from imagination is a contradiction in terms and makes frank appraisal impossible. For example, a very old wine no longer able to withstand the onslaught of oxygen might perform a dazzlingly rapid turnover in aromas as it stays in our mouth, while offering nothing for the perceptors to hold onto that would actually set the wine apart from so many others of its kind in similar condition, although we can nevertheless find every excuse to praise it for its 'great complexity.' It is the point in wine appreciation where we all might profit from the old street-corner gag teaching that what does not fit in the palm of the hand is excess. (Maybe it is to preserve their frankness, in which resides so much of their little piece of sovereignty, that all except Brillat-Savarin's "small number of the chosen few" prefer to keep their noses straight and let nuances go their way without critical comment.)

The penchant to resort to the term complexity in an omnibus way can be an especially pernicious influence on wine appreciation because it invites us to clothe subjectivity in the guise of objectivity. We typically pretend that complexity is an objectively measurable sensation, rather than recognize it as an immeasurable impression, and then with our nose to larboard we chase the fleeting nuances in our frantic effort to determine the relative complexity of the wines coming before us. As if all aromatic sensations could be named, and none would overlap, we attempt what in effect amounts to a headcount of sensations which we are ready to accept as the definitive indicator of quality:

> Complex, rich flavor with suggestions of plums, cherries, capers, violets, mint, raspberries, green pepper, almonds, cedar and an undertone of chocolate.

(Now *that* is a wine that even I know, and I am disappointed that the commentator has left out the rhubarb and bamboo shoots.) Thus distinguishing the 'extraordinarily complex' from what is only 'remarkably complex,' we convert the parade of smell associations into a rating. It is as though perception were immutable and sensation therefore knowledge – two delusions that the founding thinkers of our civilization thought they had refuted.

Being a composite impression, complexity varies from one kind of wine to another in its specific parameters, so that each type of wine has its own positive and negative features as regards complexity. Consequently, even among professional tasters only a few are so expertly versed in more than a handful of disparate wine types that they might competently hazard an opinion on the merit of relative complexity among a heterogeneous collection of wine samples. What the amateur enophile might sense and interpret as complexity in, for instance, a more or less young wine, could in the long run turn out to have been the aromatic equivalent of cacophony, with no prospect of beneficial development, which a professional taster practiced in examining that type of wine would have suspected based on past perceptions of similar wines that were in the process of becoming:

> Further one must know which odours will combine well with which, and what combination makes a good blend, just as in the case of tastes; for there too those who make combinations and, as it were, season their dishes, are aiming at the same object.

(Theophrastus, *Concerning Odours*)

The great paradox of worthy complexity is that it reaches its apogee when the aromas comprising it have pulled together, *e pluribus unum* fashion, into something surely perceptible and distinguishable. It is the complexity of those rather unified smells of nature, like that of, say, the peach, that solidly tasty fruit, which invite perusal when we are not taking them for granted.

Socrates: How about this? Is there any difference between all in the plural and all in the singular?...[The] number of the army is the same as the army, and all such cases are alike? In each of them all the number is all the thing.

Theaetetus: Yes.

Socrates: And is the number of each anything but the parts of each?

Theaetetus: No.

Socrates: Everything that has parts, accordingly, consists of parts does it not?

Theaetetus: Evidently.

Socrates: But we agreed that the all must be all the parts if all the number is to be the all.

Conundrum

Theaetetus: Yes.

Socrates: Then the whole does not consist of parts, for if it consisted
of all the parts it would be the all.

(Plato, *The Theaetetus*)

Surely wine makers seeing a bouquet well come must understand
somewhere in their being that they are challenging the immortals.

But there's another sort of complexity that has no trapdoors for us
to fall through. To seize it we need only renounce our implicit notion that
complexity can reside only in the wine itself. This notion, which is the real
menace of the complexity cult, tends to make us passive in our experience
of wine because we begin depending on the wine to engage us in a way that
is in our own power to initiate. Symptomatic of passivity is the treatment of
wine appreciation as an intellectual exercise having no emotional content.
This state of mind is marked by the attitude that this or that wine does or
does not deserve our consciousness; and it is often detectable in those of our
habitual expressions such as 'serious wine' and 'profound wine' that leave
us thinking that our only role as appreciator is to await the wine's defense of
its doctoral thesis.

If wine appreciation is to be a salutary exercise for us, complexity
is more efficaciously viewed as a condition of the taster. It is a condition
in which we feel our sensors so engaged in transmitting messages to the
perceptors of the brain, including messages possibly not realizable with
words, that we cannot derive more information about the wine without
falling back on imagination, even though our impression may be that there
would be more for the taking if only we had the time to get at it. This
condition depends less on our capacity to sense and perceive than it does on
our willingness to commune as Zorba would have us do: "In front of us now
is the pilaff; let our minds become pilaff...No half measures, you know."

In making a must of thick-skinned Complexity, let us take care not
to crack the pips: They impart an off-taste to the wine of appreciation.

*   *   *

69

12

DEATH OF A SPOIL-SPORT

It was with a collective sigh of relief this week that organized wine appreciation greeted the news of the overdue passing of maverick pundit Lucinda Rashby. Her survival to the age of 109 had been a thorn in the side of mavens who know better about which wines to toast their health with.

Rashby's coterie of diehard defenders always pointed to her inauspicious birth into a family of Bible Belt teetotalers. In her autobiography, *A Century in the Grape Thicket*, Rashby purported to have overcome this disadvantage of birth by tasting everything she could lay her hands on after being seduced over a bottle by a winery apprentice while on a proselytizing mission in Provence with her parents. She wrote that she "sometimes regretted going the wine route but had found the transition from Jesus to Dionysus as seamless as *grand vin*." Reached for comment after Rashby's death, a surviving sister said the family "had always blamed Lucinda's fall from grace on *aïoli*."

Following the Provence escapade, Rashby spent three decades wantonly drifting through winy relationships in far-flung unsung vineyards, doggedly jotting notes on the erotic effects of diverse *terroirs* that she later published under the title *Leaf Cover in Eden*. But her writing career as such did not begin until the novelty wore off in middle age. At that time she decided to settle down in Southeast Asia on the fabulous presumption that it was the ideal geographic position for anyone interested in serious 21st century punditry.

Hired as a columnist by *The Singapore Wine Grader*, Rashby gained a dubious following by rejecting Euro-centric wine appreciation and pioneering what she termed a "trans-cultural approach" to wine. Her opening salvo was fired in the incendiary article, "A Yen for Yin and Yang," in which she put forth the subversive notion that "palates trained on satay and duran are not going to have the same perceptions and reactions as mine."

Death of a Spoil-Sport

She proceeded to revamp scoring technique by awarding, for instance, the same decimal points to wines that displayed nuances of Filipino *tuba* as to those that featured nuances of French *cassis*.

But Rashby characteristically overreached herself, and the *Wine Grader* sacked her after she rejected scoring altogether and declared that "only the class of terminally unimaginative palates thirst for it." Already in her seventh decade, she moved to Fairbanks, Alaska, and began free lancing. Her treatise from that period, "A Place for Wine in the Aleut Diet," attracted particular approbation from Enophile Weight Watchers Anonymous.

Rashby's greatest career challenge came when she lost her palate at the age of 82. [Editor's Note: 22 was more like it.] She then turned to wine appreciation theory, at which time she advanced what she considered her greatest legacy, the notorious "unity of bouquet" theory, in which she argued that a wine has fully matured when it yields the same perception at any distance from the rim of the glass at which any smell can be perceived at all. A hue and cry was raised about it by other pundits, since it is precisely the instability of bouquet perception that is their bread and butter.

At the age of 94, Rashby dubiously claimed that her palate had made a miraculous comeback. But reflecting back on her extended incapacitation, she later said that what she had really lost was not her palate, but rather her stomach for endlessly groping for and spitting out the same adjectives: "How many times can one write 'lemony' or 'grassy' without becoming sated? Besides, why should anyone be that interested in what goes on in my mouth?" It was at this point that the Federation en masse became exasperated and blackballed her.

Among her other eccentricities, Rashby did not maintain a home wine cellar, which she declared to be "a lifestyle anchor that begets as many cobwebs in the mind as on the bottles." She further scandalized mainstream pundits by broadcasting that "no pundit who understands the system needs a cellar anyway since winery owners routinely curry favor by opening the best old vintages for them when they visit." Actually, her prejudice against home cellars was an obvious holdover from her sticky Singapore and frigid Fairbanks periods, or else from her earlier years of never knowing where her next bed and pantry were going to be.

Desert Island Wine

But most irksome of all to the craft was the fact that the eno-clastic Rashby far outlived her pundit contemporaries. She had rejected all of their blandishments and endorsements in favor of particular wines as aids to longevity, insisting that many of the most salubrious wines she drank resulted from the intuitive mixing of leftovers. However, in connection with another of her harebrained theories, she attributed her great age to having relied on certain categories of wine during particular stages of her life, such as bone-dry red wine in her bud-break stage in bed and bush, and semi-sweet white wine in her super-maturity on the sofa and chaise.

Fittingly, the cause of death was reported as acute phenol compound deprivation. But Rashby – a misguided rebel to the very end – succumbed only after holding out for the release of sheepskin samples from the New Millennium vintage of Georgian late-harvest Rkatsiteli-Semillon blends.

*　　*　　*

13

VINTAGE CENTURY

Thanks to advanced chrono-cybernetic technology, the following articles have been retrieved from mid-21st century media news reports about a legal case of sobering portent for wine producers, merchants and consumers, especially enophiles planning to leave wine stocks to future generations.

Item: "High Court Lowers Boom on Wine"
(*Washington NetSurfer*, Nov. 14, 2048)

In a unanimous decision, the Supreme Court today upheld the authority of Federal law enforcement agencies to confiscate statutorily excessive private stocks of wine. Anti-wine forces hailed the decision as a major victory over euphoria and ecstasy.

Writing the opinion for the Court in the case of DeBenedictis v. the United States, Chief Justice Elroy Woodprose stressed that a family environment is no excuse for the perpetuation of unwholesome habits: "The community at large has an inherent right, as inferred from the general welfare and posterity clause of the Preamble, to protection from scientifically proven retrograde customs that individuals or families may have inherited from less enlightened forebears." Woodprose cited the case of Hernandez v. the City of El Paso (2038), in which piñata games were struck down because they teach children violence towards animals.

The DeBenedictis case had its origin on December 24, 2042, when Bureau of Alternative Lifestyles and Dubious Substances (BALDS) agents, disguised as kings and shepherds, interrupted the Christmas Eve supper at the home of Felix DeBenedictis of Rahway, New Jersey. The BALDS had been alerted to numerous deliveries of suspicious looking cartons to the residence in the preceding weeks.

Desert Island Wine

DeBenedictis originally was only to be charged with corrupting the morals of youth in a family setting. But the raid uncovered nearly 9,000 bottles of wine stored in the basement of the home. This amount far exceeded the 220 bottles that would have been permissible under the Controlled Substance Abuse Act of 2027, which provided for a maximum carry-in of 100 bottles from pre-Act holdings plus 8 bottles per annum additional stockpiling thereafter. The entire DeBenedictis collection was seized immediately by the BALDS.

Today's decision effectively precludes recourse by wine users to exclusions under the Ethnic Preservation Act of 2035. Lawyers for DeBenedictis argued that their client's wines were protected under the Act because the family is of Italian Catholic origin and wine with meals is an ingrained Mediterranean Christian cultural habit. But the high court rejected both the ethnic and the sectarian claims.

The Court held that the plaintiff's ethnic contention was based erroneously on the discredited theory known as the French Paradox, which promoted twice-daily dosages of red wine as an antidote to routine gastronomic excess. The Pramnian Hyperbole was cited as "the earlier and authentic Mediterranean tradition."

Derived from data from Homeric Era Pramnian wine villages on the Aegean island of Icaria, the Hyperbole demonstrated that a proto-Mediterranean diet low in consumption of wine of any color (less than three 4-oz. draughts weekly) results in waistlines 10 percent shorter and life-spans 5 percent longer than in neo-Mediterranean diets that include wine as a mealtime commonplace. Chief Justice Woodprose emphasized that the arithmetical implications of the Pramnian findings preclude the amassing of wine beyond the currently permissible level.

Because of the Christmas Eve timing of the BALDS raid, DeBenedictis also claimed religious protection under the Ethnic Preservation Act. But the Court refuted this contention on the basis that any religious underpinning involved could only be a holdover from the polytheistic age and encourage euphoria and ecstasy, both of which are prohibited even under the exclusions of the Act.

Previously, in Cohen and Kentu v. the State of Georgia (2041), the high court had allowed the uncontrolled purchase of the generic products 'Kosher Sweet Wine' and 'Pan-African Mead' in connection, respectively, with Passover and Kwanzaa celebrations. However, those exclusions were based on expert enological testimony confirming that neither beverage was conducive either to aging and cellaring or to euphoria and ecstasy, much less to addiction.

The DeBenedictis decision already is fueling a renewed national campaign against wine. The efforts are being spearheaded by the Post-Neo-Prohibitionist wing of the Constitutional Agenda Party (CAP).

Representative Dexter Lee Washburn-Nagashima (CAP-North Carolina) told reporters today that he will shortly introduce new anti-wine legislation calling for a ban on new vineyard plantings and curtailment of Federal funding for all viti-vinicultural research and wine export promotion. While denying any retaliatory motives, Washburn-Nagashima advocates applying to wine "the same moral imperatives used by wine-sipping urban liberals to obliterate the tobacco industry in my district."

Some wine opponents are urging stronger measures in the wake of DeBenedictis. Christians Against Dionysus (CAD) is demanding that all vines within a 30-mile radius of co-ed dormitories and mixed-sex military installations be uprooted so that winery tasting rooms will not be accessible to potential sex miscreants. Speaking from the steps of the Supreme Court after today's decision, CAD spokesperson Jezebel Skinner explained, "The blatantly debauched tendencies of the pagan wine-god should alert all God-fearing people of any persuasion to wine's essential depravity."

Negative reactions to the DeBenedictis decision from pro-wine groups thus far have been vocalized primarily by the governing boards of the nation's Senior Citizen Zones. Many of the country's seniors qualified for doctors' certificates of irremediable wine addiction in connection with wine purchase easements under the Physician-Assisted Suicide Act of 2039.

Desert Island Wine

Item: "Industry in Ferment after DeBenedictis"
(*Wine Guardian*, November 20, 2048)

The wine world was rocked this week by the Supreme Court's ruling against perfectly respectable levels of home wine stocks in the DeBenedictis case.

The negative consequences were immediate and far-reaching. Old-vintage wines poured out of basements across the country as panic selling ensued. Fine wine prices declined precipitously and caused mass layoffs of sommeliers. Stock prices for the multinational provisions conglomerates that dominate the industry also nose-dived. The only positive development reported was a tripling in value of original label artwork held in public and private collections.

An emergency working tasting to console producers was organized by the Committee for the Defense of Wine and Civilization within 48 hours of DeBenedictis. In her welcoming remarks, Committee Chairperson Melissa Cruxly struck a receptive chord with her statement that "wine people have been too mellow for too long." Indeed, a great deal of producer self-criticism was heard during the tasting's first flight (from the Watery Whites category). Several attendees charged the industry with flaccid complicity in perpetuating the French Paradox myth even after it had been exposed as a salve to food abusers.

Speakers firmed up during the second flight (Over-filtered Reds) and blamed demographic developments beyond the industry's control. Some of the instances cited were nationwide phenomena, such as the rise in inter-ethnic marriages favoring rice wine, banana beer and hormonal control beverages with meals. Other examples were regional, notably the exodus of California wine drinkers to Oahu following Hawaii's legalization of mix-and-match polygamy.

The third and final flight (Stuck-fermentation Dessert Wines) was generally volatile and acerbic in its accusations against the Supreme Court and the Bureau of Alternative Lifestyles and Dubious Substances. But Jerry Grosslager, the doyen of wine retailers, told the assembly of palates that the industry should have seen the handwriting on the wall for home cellars when cigar humidors were banned by the legislation implementing the Ozone Layer Protection Treaty of 2020.

Vintage Century

As the initial shock of the DeBenedictis decision wears off, producers are trying to devise viable strategies for an embattled future. The industry leader, Consolidated Wineries, which controls 38 percent of U.S. vineyard land, held an ad hoc teleconference with its district managers, and CEO Milton Trudgemire reported afterward that Consolidated would be focusing on acreage reduction. The key issue is whether to sell off low-yielding land of high quality, which can be planted to vegetables, or high-yielding land of low quality, which can be given over to grazing. "Our dilemma," said Trudgemire, "is whether foodies prefer to take *terroir* by the root or on the hoof."

The ever innovative Windfinger Vineyards, one of the nation's leading independent wineries, is concentrating on product range. Third-generation Windfinger owner Jeb Putterman is relying on retro-technology to take up the slack. He announced that Windfinger will introduce a 'New Age' series using scientifically proven ancient Greek and Roman techniques. "These wines are wonderful for mixing with water, which clearly is where the Court is pointing us," explained Putterman. Windfinger plans to market a Thalassitis ('Sea-wine') in the classical Greek tradition, from sauvignon blanc and seawater, as soon as the National Board of Appellations and Terroirs takes a stand on the Atlantic and Pacific oceans.

Not all varietal specialists are affected equally by DeBenedictis. Gewürztraminer growers, in particular, remain bullish. The variety has continued to buck all negative trends and gain ground due to the powerful influence of the Chinese market on world export sales. Just two weeks ago, Chairman Xhin Hsin Tsin of Wok and Wine Trading Corporation in the People's Metropolis-Mall of Hong Kong stated that gewürztraminer comprises 87 percent of all Chinese imports of wine and is favored by restaurants of all regional types. Gewürztraminer already has a 43-percent share of U.S. vineyard land, including 58 percent on the West Coast alone.

Less affected producers also include those in the states of Ohio, Michigan, New York and South Carolina because of Ethnic Preservation Act exclusions pertaining to wines produced from indigenous American grapes. These wines are protected because of their large-scale purchase by the Native American Board of Entertainment Facilities for consumption on their gambling reservations.

Desert Island Wine

Reverberations of DeBenedictis are also being felt around the world. Eur-Asian Union (EAU) Commissioner for Agriculture Yevgenii Dionysievich Vinogradov, speaking candidly after the fourteenth toast at a banquet in Tbilisi, commented, "This is crushing news to the wine industry from Toulouse to Tashkent. U.S. collectors were our bread and salt. Nobody but novice Swiss bankers had as much blind faith in our *terroirs* as the Americans did." Vinogradov predicted that the EAU would be compelled to redouble its subsidies for export programs that instruct inhabitants of the Pacific Rim in the art of appreciating occidental label terminology.

Meanwhile, in the first active European reaction to DeBenedictis, the Institute of French-Only Gastronomy in Lyon announced that gewürztraminer's hold on vineyards in the province of Alsace will be targeted to reach 98 percent by 2052. The press release stated that this was motivated entirely by domestic French gastronomic developments, and "has everything to do with *choucroûte* in Alsace and nothing whatsoever to do with *bok choy* in Hunan."

Item: "Bitter Aftertaste in Rahway"
(*Here and Now Magazine*, December 2048)

Felix DeBenedictis spends hours everyday sitting alone in his empty basement and remembering better times. Here he once kept nearly 9,000 bottles of wine stored. They were seized by the Bureau of Alternative Lifestyles and Dubious Substances (BALDS) six years ago this month. Last month, the Supreme Court put its stamp of approval on the confiscation. DeBenedictis is trying to come to terms with the realization that the wines are never returning.

His troubles began on December 24, 2042, when BALDS agents raided his home in Rahway, where he has lived all his 76 years. Felix's eldest son, Jody, recalls the night. "You can't imagine what it was like. It was Christmas Eve and we had just finished the shellfish and Soave course. Then we're stormed by these BALDS guys dressed like it was Halloween. We had five more courses to go. Even the Mafia lets you enjoy a last meal before execution." Jody says the BALDS might just as well have killed his father because he was never the same after the trauma of the raid. "Pop has been inhospitable ever since. Used to be, the arrival of any guest was an excuse to pull a cork."

And that, maintains BALDS District Director Theo Axworthy, is exactly why the DeBenedictis home had to be raided. "Anybody could go into that house and tank up on a glass of wine while the old man chatted them up. Their families were being robbed of quality time and then they'd be out on the Interstate and Internet causing billions of dollars of damage to the economy." But worst of all from BALDS' perspective, Felix DeBenedictis was trying to pass his habits on to his grandnephews and grandnieces, who at the time of the raid numbered 35. "You don't have to be a Malthus," explains Axworthy, "to see the exponential implications for wine abuse in this country."

But DeBenedictis, whose lips were moistened with wine as an infant by his Italian-born great-grandfather, seems incapable of conceiving that he might be culpable for anything. "You'd think I'd been passing out cigarettes at day-care centers," he says, shaking his head in incomprehension.

About half of the seized wines were early vintages from American wineries, most of which are now defunct, and DeBenedictis claims that he would never have wasted them on youth. "I was saving them to find out whether the old pundits were right about aging times. I tried to explain that to the agents, but BALDS don't think" [sic].

Ironically, the BALDS had no idea of the scofflaw magnitude of the DeBenedictis wine collection until they entered the house and found him gathering some bottles in the basement. Axworthy compares the stash to the legendary shoe stockpile of the 20th century fetishist and Philippine strongwoman, Imelda Marcos. "When you talk about Felix DeBenedictis, you're talking about an obsessive-compulsive of the first rank. The man never saw a label he didn't want."

But DeBenedictis believes he was targeted for severe punishment because of his vociferous defense of wine drinking at his first trial in the Federal District Court of New Jersey. At that time, he challenged the worth of the Index of Statutory Intoxication (ISI), which has been lowered several times since its inception in 2015. He has not changed his views today and contends that he is a saner driver after double the minimal ISI intake than people stressed out from a day of coffee and cola while glued to their word processors. "Sure, my reactions are slowed," he argues, "but my being is also calmed and you won't find me running over people to get anywhere. A little wine is as good as *t'ai chi* and should have equal protection under the Ethnic Preservation Act."

Roberta Batdorf, the Rahway Social Services psycho-civic counselor assigned to DeBenedictis the past six years, says his statements are typical of the un-rehabilitated wine user. "People like him simply do not feel all is well with the world if they have not heard a cork pop at dinnertime."

She also observes that his preference not to drink wine by himself is consistent with the general pathology of wine users in exploiting the substance to satisfy their craving for companionship. "That's why he had to be stopped," notes Batdorf. "The truly healthy members of our society satisfy these human needs via the Internet and the Inter-screen, as well as management meetings, sports huddles and so on, where one is free to be oneself in a constructive and purposeful way."

Asked about his own habits while imbibing, Felix DeBenedictis admits to not accomplishing much of anything.

As Christmas Eve approaches, the DeBenedictis family is preparing for their traditional meal, but their patriarch will not talk about what they will drink. He only knows for sure that he will not have his collection back. "It makes me sad. I inherited a lot of those bottles from my father and feel I've let him down. He saw this day coming in this country and knew we had to stock up. He was a visionary – especially after a glass or two."

*   *   *

14

ACID REIGN

Apple of our eye, Acide,
We spied you in the garden,
Like Father Adam, we took a shine,
Suckers born for your green charm,
And telling the Gardener when we bit,
'A frisky devil made us do it.'

There must be something hormonal about it. I, at least, was most active in seeking it between the ages of 15 and 30. I am speaking of course about the darling constituent of today's wine lover: acidity.

As a child I was completely satisfied with apple juice and the way it spread its mollycoddling sensations so evenly all about my mouth and gave me a sense of well-being. But in adolescence I awoke to a need for the unsettling tang of localized sensations and found my solution in more frankly acidic beverages that pique zonally.

My experience might have to do with Aristotle's puzzlement over why men like wine but children do not. He thought it must be because men are "hot and dry," whereas children are "moist as well as hot." Acidity after all is, as Plutarch said, a 'refrigerant.' What is more, it is best served cold, like wicked revenge.

I first looked to piercing lemonade of my own bold making to satisfy my new need. Soon I was caught as well on the tines of grapefruit juice. Later, the titillating cranberry juice drinks came along and I was won over to them too. After I had become a wine drinker and was in the Navy I discovered a pomegranate juice drink and used to stow a dozen cans of it aboard ship before sailing. Subconsciously I must have been substituting it for the wine I could not have at sea. Plutarch considered pomegranates one of the 'vinous fruits.'

Desert Island Wine

The myriad configurations of the various sorts of acid no doubt motivated my curiosity about all the different kinds of wine. Wine's other constituent parts do not exercise anywhere near the degree of versatility in making themselves perceptible. Sometimes I even think that acidity, not alcohol, is the bait on the hook of the wine habit.

On you, Acide, we depend,
To keep our midriffs squarely,
Your spare figure in our chamber,
Races against lardy surfeit,
So, trim your sails and cut our fat,
We raise your glass to Ol' Jack Sprat.

Never in the history of wine was there a time when acidity was not appreciated. It may be true that the ancients were fonder of 'oily' wine than later people have been. But that was because they believed oiliness more essential than acid to wine's true nature. Acid was considered more an attribute of water, because it was thought to derive from air, or oxygen (which is helpfully translated by the Germans as *sauerstoffe*). The mixture of vinegar and water called *oxykratous* by the Greeks was a 'wine' given only to laborers.

Wine nevertheless was intuitively expected to have the uplift of acid. One of the encomiums that the Greeks bestowed on a wine was *eutonos*, or 'firm,' in alluding to the synergy of acidity and vinosity. The term was a spatial concept indicating the undergirding of the tongue. It alludes to a sensation not unlike those experienced in other body parts circumstantially.

It's Aristotelian to think that the nature of wine owes to one quality that expresses its sum or essence. Some early post-Renaissance enophiles subscribed to a make-believe constituent called *oenanthacin*, which they visualized as the winy part of wine. But now we have acidity, and it is all the more satisfying to us because of its association with salads and slimming.

Acid Reign

Acidity's rise was assisted by the serving of food in courses beginning in the 19th century. Before that time no one gave much thought to the palate cleansing sensations of acidity in wine. No one had to. Acidity was built into the meal in other ways: verjuice, lemon or vinegar in the dish; or, on the side, tartly dressed salads, or even pickles, the *aceteria* of the ancient Romans. Indeed wine did not have to be drunk for its quench at all while actually dining – and its qualities were not usually judged from that perspective.

The growing importance of acidity as a measure of wine quality may have determined the further course of wine ranking classifications that the 19th century produced. Modifications to these rankings are still being made today, and one senses acidity behind the changes. Today even firm wines can be remarked unfavorably when they are not also 'crisp.'

Acide, you are the real one,
Supple organs wag for you,
Your shrill shrieks and de Sade thrills,
Send shivers through our dull timbers,
With paper cuts and rapier thrusts,
You shade our souls an icy glaucous.

We use the tongue instinctively to raise wine to the hard palate, and we have a dual and contradictory purpose in doing it. We are trying to extract the flavor so as to enjoy and pace our imbibing, but also to divest the tongue of the foreign liquid so that it may return to its original equilibrium.

We can feel a shearing action on the wine as we pass it between the upper surface of the tongue and the hard palate, but it all happens too quickly for our faculties to describe the texture definitively. But thanks to acidity the shearing is accompanied by a physical reaction, namely the begetting of spittle, to which we can make oblique reference in distinguishing wines.

Acidity and mucus, I submit, were behind André Jullien's seminal classification of modern wines in 1816. He identified three basic types: dry (*sec*); liquorous (*de liqueur*); and mellow (*moelleux*). The dry were characterized as 'piquant.' Liquorous wines were noted for their retention

83

of sugariness. The mellow wines "without having a sugary taste, or a flat one, have a certain consistency, and are rather sweet than dry and piquant."

The dry wines are recognized when we can perceive saliva welling up under the tongue right after intake; that is, even as the tongue is just beginning to move the wine across the hard palate. The saliva then serves to maximize the rate of shear in these apparently acid-suffused wines. Jullien gave Alsatian and Rhine wines as examples.

The liquorous wines are sheared largely by the mechanical force of the tongue, helped along by residual mucus trapped in the onslaught of the unctuousness of wines apparently suffused with sweet-tasting components like sugar, alcohol and glycerin, all of which retard our perception of saliva formation. Saliva only exerts itself as the wine is being swallowed; or else after a prolonged retention that causes acid to provoke saliva until swallowing is compelled. Jullien's example was Port.

The wines called mellow are characterized by a delayed appearance of saliva, but an appearance which is perceptible while all of the wine is still in the mouth during a normal length of stay. Jullien indicated Bordeaux and Burgundy as his examples, with the latter "more mellow" than the former.

But all three of these basic conditions are subject to the caveat that as we continue sipping, saliva formation will become a self-regenerating force and will interfere with our discernment of the wine's original texture. Acidity willy-nilly grows on us.

Hone our thoughts steel bright, Acide,
To find your words of honor,
For when you set our teeth on edge,
Or brush along our damp-walled cheek,
The extra pleasure therein dwells,
To know your kiss and tell it well.

Acid Reign

Acidity's current appeal has an intellectual as well as a visceral side. I discovered this with a particular wine I came to know over a period of years. I learned that the correct way to refer to its characteristic progression through the mouth is 'pointed,' so as to indicate the transition from 'round' to 'sharp' sensations. It is our old basic cone. Because a wine has dimensions in the mouth after all.

Taking the same approach to the wine's mouth aroma and its tactile finish, I would come up with quite a fascinating schematic drawing of it. As a multi-plane diagram it could even be framed for hanging on my wall. Certainly this wine would look 'complex.'

"Every form of body," wrote Plato, "has depth: and depth must be bounded by plane surfaces." It is primarily acidity that gives geometric shape to wine. Although acid was regarded by the ancients as belonging essentially to the element of water, it was also considered to partake of the element of fire, to which wine was linked.

Acid's Greek name was *oxys*, or 'sharp.' Its straight-edge quality accounts for angular or irregular shapes in liquids. Plato remarked that things are called 'hard' or 'soft' depending on whether or not the flesh yields to them: "Those which yield are such as have a small base of support; and the figure with square surfaces, as it is the most firmly based, is the most stubborn form." Nothing tells it better in wine than the word by which the Greeks called the driest wines, *austeros*, or 'austere.'

Acidity these days is giving rise to a bevy of terms by which to box in our response to wine. The enological troopers are even coming up with all the terms needed for a Euclidian enometry: square, angular, convex, oblong, rectilinear, etc. The conceptual and practical problems facing today's enophile could seem like kid stuff to our grandchildren. I do not envy their pondering whether to serve a rectangular wine with an oblong food.

Acide, your blue blood courses,
Quirks become your chiseled face,
For far above the soil you're borne,
Never to long for humble earth,

Desert Island Wine

But with your breeding from the sky,
You alone do string our spirits high.

Were we somehow to spread out humankind's experience with wine chronologically for viewing and consideration, we should have to divide it into two great epochs: the Unsalted Era and the Salted Era. Acidity proves it.

Athenaeus, alluding to a very old oral tradition, related an early time when salt was not used in Greece. He also mentioned that a priestly prohibition against the use of salt on sacrificial meat continued into his own day. This suggests a lengthy transition period between the Unsalted and the Salted eras.

Salt may finally have needed the aura of heavenly approval since Plutarch said it is one of the common things people liked to call 'divine.' Salt's virtue, he explained, is its usefulness in adapting food to the body. His companion Symmachus observed further that "moderately salty foods… bring out the sweetness and smoothness of any kind of wine."

If there be anything at all to our assumption that food habits influence tastes in wine, then surely the Unsalted and the Salted eras would each have their own characteristic wines. And those of the Unsalted Era would have been peculiarly suited to the tastes of virgin palates never touched by salt. For salt, we know today, takes the edge off acidity.

The transition from the old epoch to the new must have been a period of confused habits that enabled wine styles from the Unsalted Era to survive into the Salted Era. Suspected kinds of wine can be recognized as those which inherently 'lack acidity.' But there remains one nagging question: Would not the less acidic wines of the Unsalted Era have a 'natural superiority' over those made for the skewed palates of the Salted Era?

*   *   *

The following is a translation of a recently discovered, previously unknown dialogue of Plato. Its authenticity has been disputed in wine circles, where the message was found unpalatable, but it is included here anyway for the sobering inspiration of Attica that it offers.

15

AMPHOROTHIRAS

Characters of the dialogue:

Socrates
Amphorothiras
Kratereus

The dialogue takes place at Amphorothiras's stall at the market-place of Athens.

Kratereus: You are perfectly right, Amphorothiras. This is quite marvelous wine, every bit deserving of the prized '5 grape clusters' you awarded it in your announcement of new arrivals. And I see what you mean about its having an elusive taste of arbutus berries. No wonder my fellow Areopagites have recommended it so highly. I only hope it is not too late for you to have ten jars available for me.

Amphorothiras: I should see to it that it is never too late for a preferred customer such as yourself. I will have the ten jars readied for you at my storehouse at the Piraeus this very day, if you wish, and you may send a man to cart them away as early as tomorrow morning. You have made an excellent choice, my friend – but the producer of this wine never makes wine of less than '5 grape cluster' quality. This sweet-drinking potation has all that a wine could offer and more, and will provide you years of enjoyment, Kratereus. Just be sure, as always, to keep the jars stored upright in a cool dark place.

Kratereus: I can manage that quite well at my villa by Pentelicus, and ...

Amphorothiras: Well, well, of all ... Would you believe it? Please, pardon my rude interruption, Kratereus. But, if my eyes do not deceive me, it is

Desert Island Wine

Socrates who is approaching there. Now comes a challenge for a purveyor of choice wines! – a fellow who can hold his own with the best of them when the cup starts going round, but whose palate is a bit too far removed from his brain to judge the worth of what he is tasting.

Socrates, is that you? What a pleasure to see you here before my stall. Could it be that you have come to inquire about the recently arrived wine from Thasos? I can personally vouch for the scrupulous methods of its production: Fiber did not touch this wine. [The allusion apparently is either to an ancient method of filtration or to goatskin wine containers. MLG] And it was such an outstanding vintage, this one. Why, this wine is bursting with galaxies of flavors known and unknown. My friend Kratereus here has just purchased ten jars. Only, please, do allow me to pour you a cup, so that you might judge for yourself.

Socrates: Ten jars, is it? I am in enough trouble at home as it is. A purchase of that magnitude would hardly persuade my wife to water the wine of her discontent. As for the sample, Amphorothiras, you would do better to keep it for another passerby, one with greater discernment by which to make the distinctions you would have me make. Nor am I entirely sure as to just what it is in this wine that will suit me more on the inside than does the one from Kalolineas by Pentelicus, to which I am accustomed, although I see that on the outside I would have the '5 grape clusters.'

Kratereus: Kalolineas? I believe he is just down the road from my villa. But the poor fellow must never have been listed here at Amphorothiras's stall, for if he had been I certainly would know him and his wine.

Amphorothiras: I appreciate your circumstances, Socrates, and your condition as well. Let me assure you that I have never sold any man wine that he does not want. My trade is not without its nobility, after all. I seek only to provide my customers a good worthy of their enjoyment, and to do so at a fair price, no matter that I handle no wine that is not up to '3 grape cluster' quality.

Socrates: Your reputation has made the rounds of the market-place, Amphorothiras, and indeed of all Athens, and Attica beyond. Even Kalolineas now has no greater ambition than to be awarded three of your

Amphorothiras

'grape clusters.' Please, though, do go on, that I might learn from yourself about the nature of the service you wish to render me.

Amphorothiras: It is certainly no trifling one. Many customers for wine want a guide to whom they may refer confidently before risking a purchase. Therefore, I do for them that which they cannot see to for themselves. I make it my business to taste more wines than anyone else; and every two years I make a wine journey all around the Aegean. On my last circuit alone I tasted one-thousand different wines from three-hundred producers on the mainland and islands. How would, say, my friend Kratereus here, learn of all those wines and know which ones to seek were it not for me? Why, he would have to desert his livelihood and family, not to mention his indispensable civic functions, to find the wines I bring him – and then he likely would not even be able to afford those any longer. Further, he would not, for all his trouble, find finer wines than those I select.

Kratereus: Quite so. Why, I am so busy at the Court of the Areopagus that I have no time to train my palate as I should like to do. (And am I any better of eye, nose and hand when it comes to choosing anything else for the table? My ears are still ringing from the shrill chastisement my wife delivered me just yesterday for the mullet that were sold to me at the Piraeus.) Yes, I am better off, Socrates, leaving all to Amphorothiras. No other opinion in the market-place has as much credibility as his does. What wine is there that he does not know?! One-thousand wines tasted on just one journey! No wonder Amphorothiras always knows what will suit me.

Socrates: Your tasting forays do inspire awe here in the market-place, Amphorothiras. Nonetheless, I should like to learn what you gain from the one-thousand wines that Kratereus would not be able to gain from any one of them.

Amphorothiras: Experience and knowledge, of course.

Socrates: Are you saying that tasting wine is a species of thought from which knowledge is deduced?

Amphorothiras: You tease me, Socrates. It seems that just a whiff of my stall can tickle even you. No, I am not saying such a thing at all. Obviously, the palate lies apart from the brain. But, by whatever connection there is between palate and brain, tasting does give rise to thought, which in turn allows understanding.

Socrates: What is it that you would understand?

Amphorothiras: What else but quality? By what else should I choose my wines and assign my 'grape cluster' rankings for the good of my clientele?

Socrates: The word 'quality' certainly hangs thickly over the market-place.

Amphorothiras: It is fitting to speak of the market-place, Socrates. Wine is no different from any other good sold here. For there are specific standards of quality by which to judge it.

Socrates: I should like to know, then, what the so called standards of quality represent.

Amphorothiras: They of course mark off the attributes specific to wine. For instance, there is 'bouquet.'

Socrates: And the sum of the standards necessarily must amount to what is recognized by one and all as wine. Is that so?

Amphorothiras: It could be nothing else but wine; when all those attributes are present, we know that it is wine.

Socrates: Therefore, each of the standards must be applied equally to each sample of wine.

Amphorothiras: Yes, and I taste all wines democratically, as it were. How else should I preserve my integrity and reputation in the market-place?

Kratereus: You can take my word for it, Socrates. Nobody can match Amphorothiras for consistency. When he offers a wine of '5 grape cluster' quality, his customers can rest assured that they will find that quality in the jar. Why, if memory serves me, I have even discerned the flavor of arbutus berries in practically all of Amphorothiras's '5 grape cluster' selections.

Amphorothiras

Socrates: Then every wine that meets the standards must be wine equally, the one neither more nor less than the other. Do you agree?

Amphorothiras: I would not go that far, Socrates. For in fact, the specific characteristics do differ from wine to wine, so that quality in all that qualifies as wine cannot always be manifested equally. Indeed, if it were otherwise, people would have no need of my service, and my 'grape cluster' rankings would have no meaning.

Socrates: Just when I thought we were making port, a fickle wind has blown us back out to sea, Amphorothiras. You are now saying that even if all the samples have the quality of wine, quality may vary by degree among them. You must be speaking, then, of some other kind of quality.

Amphorothiras: Well, one must additionally judge quality by reference to specific kinds of wine which, being recognized as paragons of quality, serve as models against which to evaluate all others. For example, we have the model of Thasian wine, which has enjoyed its reputation for who knows how long – since the time of Homer, perhaps. And it is exactly this knowledge of the models that my experience provides me.

Socrates: Now I am at a loss to understand what these models, as you call them, might add to an examination of quality once it is perceived that all the qualities of wine are present in all the samples.

Amphorothiras: Quite simply, they enable me to lead my clientele in the right direction of their inclination, and exactly, I might add, to the extent that the individual customer values and can pay for his preference.

Socrates: In that case, I should like to know by what means you reconcile their preference, if that is what it is, with the various models.

Amphorothiras: By memory. I have developed, as a result of my experience, a very keen memory for tastes, such that I can instantly recall specific wines and their place in enology. As soon as a customer tells me something of the sort of flavor he seeks, I know precisely the jars he should sample.

Kratereus: And none below '3 grape cluster' quality!

Desert Island Wine

Socrates: But you are describing the situation in which memory begets only a notion, not knowledge.

Amphorothiras: Well, however you want to call it, Socrates, without me my clientele should do no more than head down the road, pitcher in hand, to fill up with Kalolineas's 'no cluster' stuff. Anyway, now that I have satisfied your curiosity about my experience and services, may I show you my list?

Socrates: Since you purport to deal with what is true and unchanging, Amphorothiras, you should not confuse your experience with knowledge. The conclusions that you have drawn from your tasting experience have nothing to do with truth, but instead are concerned with what is temporal. Just so, we may take the example of Thasian wine and anticipate a time when it will have been replaced by some other wine as a reputed paragon of quality, or rather, that 'quality' in which the market-place deals. People then will speak of it as lesser in quality than some wines that now could never approach its price, when actually it will only be different from those. From this it is plain that, since no manifestation of quality has all qualities, it is left to the market-place, and the forces that persuade it now this way and now that, to decide at any moment which qualities are to be preferred over others. Since it is only against that 'experience and knowledge' that your 'grape clusters' and the rest of your services have any meaning, and since my own palate falls beyond their range, it is 'no sale,' Amphorothiras.

*　　*　　*

16

SKIMMING THE FROTH

"There is no air in the world like the air of Maine, and Eden's air is like champagne."

The folks who settled Eden, Maine, in 1796, must have been bubbling over with enthusiasm for their new community when they came up with their proselytizing rhyme for the place. But the incantation of Champagne's name as an unabashed expression of pleasure was something almost as new to the world then as Eden itself. Champagne had been known only as a still wine until the 18th century, and the introduction of the sparkling kind around that time met with prolonged hesitation in the market at large, and with outright antipathy from old-school enophiles. In 1775, just two decades before Eden's founding, the English enophile-historian-author Edward Barry reckoned that the growing popularity of the "frothy" kind of Champagne was but a passing fad. Nor did he disguise his relief that the French "have almost entirely quitted that depraved taste." But the reality was contrary to Barry's wishful observations on consumer preferences. In fact the Eden jingle of 1796 serves to mark the time when carbonic gas burst forth in triumph over the last bastions of resistance.

Barry might sound distinctly odd from our perspective over two centuries later. Nowadays we are so perfectly at ease with bubbly drinks by such a very tender age that a positive response to carbonic gas becomes second nature to us and deludes us at an older age into thinking that such a response is instinctual. But writing in our own time, the enologist Émile Peynaud lends Barry moral support by calling the taste for sparkling wine "recent and artificial" (*Le Goût du Vin*). Thus confronted by a contemporary authority, we may want to blame some shortcoming in still Champagne wine, such as excessive acidity, which made it so much more palatable as sparkling wine. But we should not dodge the real issue by our crafty externalizations.

Certainly no one can accuse us of not looking past our nose as far as effervescence is concerned. The nose is meant in part to warn us away from what might be less than salubrious for us to consume, yet we rush headlong into liquids suffused with bubbles that burst ominously on our nostrils' doorstep. Our willingness is not necessarily evidence of atrophy in the human sense of smell. Nor would it be a wholly satisfactory explanation of our fearlessness to say that our internal alarm system is not triggered when we are pleased by aroma, as we likely will be in the case of good sparkling wine. Our equally happy intake of almost anything effervescent suggests that there is more to it than the nose can tell. Most likely it is something visual.

The ancient Greeks were fascinated by the sight of comestibles that frothed. For instance, the naturalist Theophrastus rarely made specific culinary references but made an exception in mentioning "a foaming dressing" for salads which was produced by pounding a certain kind of garlic until its liquid volume increased by intake of air (*Concerning Odours*). Apparently he found it a remarkable sight and expected that his readers also saw it that way. Plato, too, came at effervescence in the first instance from its visual aspect, in referring to "capsules containing air" (*Timaeus*). He also observed that these capsules can be either "of pure moisture and transparent," in which case they are called "bubbles," or else "of earthy liquid" that has foamed up in an extensive mass, which is the peculiarity of fermentation and therefore is called by that name (*zymosin*). It was because of the visual carry-over of foam from fermentation that the Greeks gave their more or less sudsy beer the name *zythos*.

But the Greeks were skittish about carbonic gas where wine was concerned. They were well acquainted with the foam cap on fermenting wine and suspected its purity. Plutarch even reported that vintage workers were "afraid to pilfer the must while it is still fermenting" (*Table-talk*). Consequently the Greeks also had doubts about the wholesomeness of wine that was not still. There is a rare passage from Timotheus, in the 4th century B.C., suggesting that wines occasionally were tried in an ultra-fresh state while still displaying some carbonic gas commotion: "into it he poured one ivy-wood cup of red drops ambrosial bubbling with foam [*afro*]." But the only solid basis for interpreting Timotheus to mean actual rather than just metaphoric effervescence is that the modern Greeks call sparkling wine *afrodis*, or 'foamy.'

It is with good reason that we think of the ancient goddess Aphrodite. Born on the evanescent fingertips of the breakers, Aphrodite ('foam-risen') depended on the visual to captivate, and indeed she could do it like nobody's business. She was seduction personified: "The Goddess of Love and Beauty, who beguiled all, gods and men, alike; the laughter-loving goddess...who stole away even the wits of the wise" (Edith Hamilton, *Mythology*).

The Greeks attributed a goddess of such charm to sea foam because they had once thought that the foam could of itself generate life. A minute fish called *afritis*, or 'foam-fish,' was thought to be created by the thick sea foam which was observed to follow hard rains over the sea. The conceptualization of Aphrodite's birth was but a few splashes beyond that.

Plutarch mentioned that the Greeks at one time had considered it unnatural and scandalous to eat fish. In accounting for this reluctance, he cited Anaximander's theory "revealing the fish as the common father and mother of mankind" who nurtured us until we were ready to come ashore. This general theme has been more comprehensible since Darwin – might we suppose that he read Plutarch? – and his version of the evolution of our species, which is a theory that can explain why few sights entrance us as do the collapsing crests and breaking waves of the sea. It might even be said that our eye has a 'natural taste' for sea foam – surely Darwin and Anaximander would think so – or at least if compared to the foaming swirls that lure us into the strange waters of a Jacuzzi. This attraction evidently also carries over into our view of frothing drinks and causes us to run roughshod over our nose in our desire to have our senses immersed in them.

Our nature is such that we want to devour – or else be devoured by (as the case might be) – what is visually fascinating, if at all possible. Sometimes we cannot even be restrained by suspected unwanted consequences. Our nature in this respect is illustrated by such figures as Rapunzel's mother and the Eve of Garden of Eden notoriety. But just how we go about trying to consume the desired object is determined by our reckoning of it in relation to our sensory apparatus. In the case of what looks edible or drinkable we generally attempt to consummate consumption through the mouth. However, external consumption, which perhaps is a perversion of already suspect 'conspicuous consumption,' is also attempted sometimes, as in the ancient practice of olive oil applications to the body, and the modern frolic – more natural than a Jacuzzi? – of giving naughty ladies Champagne baths.

Desert Island Wine

Visually transfixed, and with our fish-man's ear tuned to the crackle, we bring the glass of bubbly liquid to our lips with as much abandon and glee as when we dive into the roaring surf at ocean's end. As soon as the carbonic gas enters the chamber of the mouth, it begins to disengage on the surfaces and we immediately notice its peculiar sensation. Peynaud called this sensation "brutal," presumably because, in Plato's words, it "corrodes the flesh by burning." But we learn to rejoice in this savor nonetheless as a boost to the spirit, a pick-me-up. This physio-psychological reaction is remarkable because of our readiness to endure a momentary shock to the nervous system. Apparently we are driven by the illusion that something is being done to quench our thirst in a way more positive than water.

We know instinctively that only water quenches real thirst, the kind of thirst which the early gastronome Brillat-Savarin termed "habitual" and "latent" because it is "part of our very existence." But in our age of hurried lifestyles, when no gratification can be sufficiently instantaneous, water's unrivalled capacity to effect quenching does not seem to do the trick for us. Because water must be swallowed if we are to feel that something is being done to resolve our condition and restore our physiological equilibrium. But let us just charge water or any other potable liquid with carbonic gas and we have the impression straight away that we are being relieved. Thus imagining that the quenching even of habitual thirst takes place in the mouth cavity, rather than deep within the body, we entertain the false hope that a liquid other than water will accomplish water's unique function.

We are all the more apt to resort to this pseudo-quenching at mealtime. Our attention then is focused on the mouth cavity, and we mistake for 'quenching' what is only a periodic alleviation of stress while the mouth performs the initial processing of solid food. Carbonic gas enjoys the advantage in satisfying this "recent and artificial" need of ours on the strength of the same rambunctious sensation that causes us to expect real physiological quenching. As a result, many wines that once would have been made to be as still as possible can only compete on today's beverage market by tickling our palate with at least a slightly noticeable spritz. We have come a long way since Eden.

*　　*　　*

17

This presentation is meant to forestall any impression left by Chapter 3 that since European fiction had not suffered from the temperance movement, it had not been impoverished. European authors themselves, for whatever reasons, sometimes removed wine-related passages. Several persons kindly supplied translations from drafts they found in antiquarian shops abroad. Three samples are offered below by way of a...

CONTINENTAL ANTIPHONE

THE SUFFERINGS OF YOUNG WERTHER (Johann Wolfgang von Goethe, 1774)
  First Book
  Time Period: 1771

The following entry originally was to have been included in the compendium of letters to Wilhelm that chronicle Werther's slide toward suicide over his romantic obsession, the dark-eyed Lotte, who is committed to her husband, the sensible businessman Albert, though she feels a physical attraction for the increasingly unstable and frustrated artist:

"August 28. Evening.

"You will forgive the haste with which I write, for I must record these notes while all is still fresh in my feverish brain. And I must be frank, Wilhelm, in proclaiming that I am still heady from imbibing wine and Lotte – I cannot separate the two; and it need not be one of those Either-Or propositions that you are so fond of posing.

"You will realize from my earlier note that this evening's dinner was in honor of my birthday. It was intended to follow upon the gift of the Wetstein edition of Homer, so tidily tied with Lotte's pink ribbon, which Albert gave me this morning. Count von R., Professor S., and Ambassador B. had been invited for the express purpose of making the rare Dionysian contributions that they were in a unique position to offer, so as to lend a Homeric air to the dinner. You can imagine the rapturous feeling that came over me when I understood that Lotte herself had arranged this. She is certainly an angel sent from the Almighty, and it is only a matter of time

– whether in this world or the next – do not be discomfited that I find little difference – until we shall be united.

"Ambassador B. was insistent that we try his wine even before sitting down to dinner. He had obtained some Chian wine while posted in Constantinople; and I was nearly beside myself when he said that it was none other than latter-day Pramnian of the sort served to Ulysses by Circe. It came as an inexpressibly precious balm to my heart, though the Ambassador, who is as ignorant of Homer as of art, was aghast when I asked Lotte for some dry biscuit and old cheese to crumble into the wine; and he was but slightly soothed by my explanation that such was Circe's habit with Pramnian – I can assure you that it was all Greek to the Ambassador. Albert deftly calmed the situation by ushering all of us to the table.

"The viands were from Lotte's garden and henhouse – tended by her personally! Oh! how I feasted on them! I cannot describe the feeling I had of being nourished by her hand. And she had alluringly flavored her cabbage dish with a red spice which Count von R. had acquired from his friend Prince E. in Vienna. It was referred to as Turkish pepper and Hungarian pepper, but whatever its origin, it should not be ingested by persons of an ardent nature. As Lotte had doubtlessly foreseen, it ignited my sentiments from head to toe. I did not miss her culinary signal; and I reached my foot under the table and touched hers as if by accident; but I believe she has begun to see this little game of mine for the sophomoric flirtation that it is.

"My sensations were only augmented by the wine, a specially prepared and aged Macedonian wine that the Count called Melenikion, with which he is supplied by a Greek merchant at Vienna, who informs him that wine of similar kind was brought by sea to fortify Agamemnon's troops at Troy! A most refreshing fragrance – *in qualitate*, to be sure – rose up from the glass; and I nearly swooned from the heavenly ecstasy, whether from the wine or the cabbage dish – there is another impossible Either-Or for you.

"We finished the entirety of the Melenikion – (I could have accomplished it alone, for many a time in the throes of some elated or dejected mood I have been seduced by a glass of far less storied wine into finishing the bottle) – but not without unfortunate effect, for Ambassador B. for no coherent reason began expounding pedantically upon the Balkan situation and the Treaty of Passerowitz and his father's part in formulating it. Albert brought it to a close by suggesting that Lotte bring in the cake

– for even adults are governed completely by cake. A marvel of a cake it was, too! – and Lotte had used in it the very pears that she and I had plucked from her tree! It was a morsel of bliss for one headed for the abyss of an early grave.

"As if to encourage us on to devour the cake, Professor S. poured a wine from Ithaca that he had brought back from his recent classical tour of Italy and Greece. I experienced from it the most unalloyed joys! A fantasm enveloped me, I tell you, and I was as among Penelope's suitors in the great hall of Ulysses's palace. Oh! to have lived in those patriarchal times. And the gleaming darkness of the wine was matched by Lotte's sparkling orbs across the candlelight. I might have gone on in this state of grace for hours, but parsing and quibbling of epic proportion arose as to whether the wine was in its bronze age or its iron age, until finally Ambassador B., whose acquaintance with Ovid is utterly rudimentary, interjected that the discussion was moot because our present-day Ithaca might not be the same isle as Homer's Ithaca. Alas, dear Wilhelm, is it my fate to be nagged by dolts of his stripe as long as I walk this firmament? I do not know how much longer I can bear it, for every day my leaves turn yellow and it grows clearer that I shall have to wait like Penelope to be joined with my beloved."

*   *   *

NOTES FROM UNDERGROUND (Fyodor Dostoevsky, 1864)
Part One, Chapter VI
Time Period: 1840-1864

After mentioning an acquaintance of his who had been a great admirer of Château Lafite, and because of it had died "with a triumphant conscience," the narrator relates some of his own experience with wine and food, in the course of explaining his contempt for himself and his times, and incidentally demonstrating his rationality:

"You never imagined me drinking Lafite, gentlemen? I only do so at the Hôtel de Paris, if you want to know. Besides, I am no connoisseur of it like he was. No, I refuse to clank my sword about Lafite. Well, but even if I had told you about it you would say that I, an insect, could not appreciate it. Of course, I would agree with you. Why, Caucasian wines used to be good enough for me. If I thought about it at length, I should no doubt think they are still more to my taste, and indeed to *le goût russe généralement*, but why should I think about it at all? The truth is that I am scarcely worth a winemaker's pause in thought. What else should you think of someone who gets drunk just as readily on Lafite as on Kakhetia? Please just think of me as an insignificant entity, a ridiculous Schleswig-Holstein struggling to breathe the same air as the great empires.

"Furthermore, since I am now forty and think I might still be here ranting and pestering you twenty years from now, I must also confess that I am not at all convinced that the Kakhetia does not do better by me in the long run than does the Lafite. I am therefore in agreement with you that it would be perfectly just if the French – and the Caucasians too, for that matter – would reserve the dregs for me. I am a worm by nature, or at least I have long thought that I should be a worm. Certainly I am a petty functionary bereft of rationality and a capacity to appreciate "the sublime and the beautiful," as we used to call it. The right thing would be to leave me in my *milieu*, the dregs.

"You may have noticed, by the way, that I hide myself in the corner and drain the last of the Sauternes bottles at the Easter buffets. Every decent man in our age must be a coward. I assure you that tossing back Sauternes is not my idea of resurrection. Bah! A despicable ant has no right to think of resurrection. It is more my idea of crucifixion, in fact. An ant needs the chaos of the five senses to undo his belief in two plus two make four and all the other insufferable and insolent "laws of nature," so as to break his inexorable march. That is why I go to the corner and plunge all at once into the dark, subterranean, loathsome petty vice of swilling Sauternes. The plain fact is that my place in life has been determined over these past forty years, and that rather than pretend to aspire to a higher position by daintily sipping Sauternes from glasses, I might just as well guzzle directly from its commercial receptacle until I am back down where I belong.

"But let us be totally honest for a change and admit that the fops who rave about the Easter *paskha* [cheese confection] are little better, standing beside the table and smacking their lips over the *paskha* mound and then pretending to imbibe Sauternes ever so preciously over the fat that is still glistening on their lips, when they are really sucking in mouthfuls at a rate hardly slower than me. I might add, too, *mes frères*, that you were just the same when Imperial Tokay was on the table not so many years ago, though now you say that you prefer to have a less unctuous and astringent wine flood the *paskha*. I have no right to an opinion on that, but until the Sauternes arrived you used to say that the Tokay looked so pretty beside the *paskha*. I always agreed with that, of course; because what other opinion should a worm have? And I was, moreover, a worm who could see color even in vodka and was quite happy drinking that with the *paskha* twenty years ago.

"But I am a babbler and surely you think that I should not be speaking this way since I have never even had the privilege of watching you drink Lafite from crystal while you are seated comfortably and the veal tongue is being sliced. That is true enough, but I saw you drinking Kindzmarauli out of crystal while eating veal brains just several years ago, and I do not imagine that you have taken a new approach. But let us recognize that I am a bureaucrat who makes it his duty to annoy and frustrate the public. It is a "law of nature." That is precisely why I demand to hear your excuse for slurping Sauternes with *kulebiaka*. There is no unctuousness to the dish at all, and yet you used to drink Tokay with it, but now you speak about the *foie gras* that lately has been added to the dish, and thus do you justify your switch to Sauternes. But I do not swallow that, and besides, I must grill you on the subject of Russian *kulebiaka*, not that recipe of Carême's which they have begun to serve in Petersburg of late. Even a functionary needs to have some grip on realities. *Point d'honneur* even for a worm, after all. And do forgive my digression."

*   *   *

THE STRANGER (Albert Camus, 1947)
  Part One, Chapter 4
  Time Period: *circa* 1938

Meursault sketches the evening when his new girlfriend, Marie, cooked for him in her Algiers apartment several days after his mother's [Maman's] funeral, and the day before he was propelled by incidental but overwhelming psycho-physical circumstances to gun down an Arab assailant of his neighbor, Raymond:

Desert Island Wine

"Marie wanted to take me to her place and cook something and have some wine. She said that if I was going to marry her I should at least know she can cook meals and choose wine. It really didn't matter whether she could or couldn't, but I stopped myself just in time from saying so out loud, and replied simply that she should not go to any trouble. Marie said she had learned to make couscous with summer vegetables and steamed fish from an Arab woman some years ago and that it was no trouble, and that in any case she had already bought wine. For some reason she added that I could probably do with a good home-cooked meal after all those lunches at Céleste's after I had put Maman in the old people's home in Marengo. I told her I doubted that I could tell the difference between what was home-cooked and what was cooked at Céleste's, and that even if I could it probably would make no difference either to my head or my digestion anyway. She looked like she didn't believe me, so it occurred to me to say that food and wine did not interest me much because Maman had not been much of a cook, even though I had not held that against Maman and didn't now either. Marie gave me a coy smile and pulled me by the arm to catch the tram for her place.

"Her apartment was two floors below the roof, and that was a relief since the accumulated warmth of the sun in top floor flats in Algiers can bring a stifling and dizzying sensation to my head. And even though the location was inland, I could catch a whiff of the sea when the breeze would blow in from the open balcony. I mentioned the breeze and the sea to Marie, just to say something nice about her apartment, and she said she was glad because it might give me an appetite for fish. This took me by surprise because I would never have guessed that had anything to do with it. Before thinking better of it I responded that I could detect the sea at my apartment too and that I was sure that blood sausage had been just as much to my taste there as fish might be in her apartment this evening. She laughed and called me a confirmed bachelor.

"Marie set the table and brought out the food, and then she asked whether I wanted white wine or red. I told her I would drink whatever she wanted. She grinned and I had no idea what could be funny until she disappeared for a moment and brought out a white Meursault from Burgundy. She giggled as she announced the name and it was obvious she was trying to amuse me with a wine bearing my own name. But I felt nothing in particular about it so I just tried to humor her by asking what she'd have done if I had

102

wanted red. She said she had also bought a red Meursault and I said I didn't know there was a red kind. Marie said I had spent too little time in France and too much time baking by the Sahara. I didn't know what to say to that, because I had not spent a lot of time on the European French side of the Mediterranean. But when she continued and said that wine deserves more attention than I give it, I pooh-poohed the idea, and without so much as a thought said, 'No.' I sensed from the pout on her lower lip that this was a mistake, and I quickly added that she could take wine as seriously as she liked.

"Afterward we went to bed. When we got up Marie asked whether I wouldn't like to leave Algiers and live with her a while in Paris. I told her we could do that if she wanted to. She refilled our glasses with the rest of the Meursault, and clinked mine with hers. Then she looked at the glasses and said the wine was elegant. I told her I didn't know what she was talking about but that I wasn't too unhappy with the wine. She said I seemed to be completely at home with Algerian wine, if I did not actually prefer it. I said I really had no preference about it but that I probably drink more wine from Dahra than anywhere else because a merchant down the street from me stocks his brother's wine from there. She called Dahra red wine 'Saharan sandpaper' and said I should be more discerning. Apparently for emphasis she added that if she had me over for a meal again she might just as well get some blood sausage wrapped in greasy paper because it suits Dahra. Maybe she expected me to be piqued and speak up for Dahra, because she seemed surprised when I answered that blood sausage and Dahra would be alright if that's what she wanted to serve me. She said I was peculiar and that she might have to rethink our relationship, but I didn't know what that meant, either, so this time I said nothing.

"On the way home I stopped off for a bottle of Dahra to drink with Raymond. Sandpaper or not, it has gone down swimmingly every time after Marie. It somehow recalls our days at the beach and our lovemaking, and makes me want to have her again, which I can't say about the Meursault. Maybe I should have told her that, but I hadn't thought of it at the time."

*   *   *

18

CONCERNING CLARRET & BOTARGO

As if wine were not a sufficiently perplexing aesthetic realm for the many still on the outside, hardly anyone coming to wine today is spared either received wisdom or extemporaneous confabulation about the proper marriage of wines and foods. Exposure to the subject is accepted among clusters within the upper middle class as being intrinsic to the initiation rites of wine appreciation. Yet the premeditated question of 'what goes with what' is of very recent posing, while as a topic for expansive wine commentary it does not antedate our own generation.

*

Pre-20th century gastronomic literature had many concerns, but wine-food combination was not one of them. Not even Brillat-Savarin addressed it as such, and that was already 1825. Instead, what little is known of early notions on the subject comes from offhand notations, most of which are found in diaries and fiction, and relate mostly to the haphazard appearance of particular wines and foods at the same table. Only the slimmest pickings are to be had in the way of references to intentional combinations. A typical observation was that of the Duke of Chandos in the early 18th century: "dry mountain Malaga [when] very old and perfect is mighty good to drink a glass of with fruit" (the Duke did not specify which fruits). Thus, the old written record does not provide historical evidence to justify thinking of the so called 'classic' combinations as ingrained cultural habits of very long standing.

The apparent laxity of our enophile predecessors may be explained in part by their rather gay view of wine's role at the table. Wine for them was less an object for critical evaluation while dining than for enjoyment. This lightheartedness must have grown out of a thankfulness which precluded questions that might be raised in times such as ours when abundance is taken for granted by anyone who can afford to be an enophile. Even further from our contemporary view, wine was treated as just another component of diet, not as something to be catered to. To the extent that a wine's properties were considered in relation to food, physiological and health effects usually took precedence. In 1602, for instance, William Vaughan recommended that red wine follow upon fish for the sake of digestive benefit. His sensibilities were still in keeping with Hippocrates's ancient prescriptions involving wine.

The general circumstances of wine imbibing have changed substantially during the past century and a half. The well-to-do of earlier times did not regale themselves with banquets of ordered courses, but instead delighted in repasts of multiple dishes and libations that spoke of a plentitude they knew to be precarious. This is not to say that diners in those times could not or did not notice differences in flavor that resulted when a particular wine came after a particular food. Rather, theirs was not a dining situation conducive to coming to fast and solemn judgments about the worth of those differences, especially not when there were other entertainments or diversions to be occupied with during a meal, as was their preference.

The condition of upper class dining began to change only with the adoption of the *service à la Russe* in Western Europe during the 19th century. Although this manner of serving originally consisted of several courses composed of several dishes each, it became customary during the second half of the century to serve only one dish per course. Enophiles adapted their wine selections accordingly, so that only one wine would appear with each course. This new habit gave the crucial impetus to forethought about the appropriateness of specific wines for particular dishes. Consequently, our 'classic' combinations, far from having anything like universal gustative validity, less gloriously are only circumstantial combinations invented by the self-conscious elite in a few places over a short span of years lasting from the late 19th century until the interwar period of the 20th century.

With the spreading affluence characteristic of the post-Second World War years in industrial countries, the upper middle class was drawn to wine connoisseurship, and with that, wine-food combination came into full flower. Wine writers grew in number, and the proliferation of wine columns and periodicals in the popular press required varying the standard fare of commentary on individual wines and regions. Wine-food combination was one topic to fill the bill in meeting the increased demands placed on wine writing. With an audience eager for all that could be offered, the subject of combinations proved a prolific source of creative punditry.

But 'combining' was also a participatory pastime that lent itself as exceptionally fine grist for home thought-mills of the wine initiates themselves as they gathered together to sniff corks and have 'a learning experience.' With a cornucopia of wines and foods available widely at all times of the year, home wining-and-dining turned into a primary leisure pursuit for some, and wine-food combination became a cerebral dining room game that took the place of the music, song, dance and general chatter of the special dining experience of earlier times. Academic courses on the subject are now being offered as well, and these are becoming compulsory for earning degrees in gastronomic studies.

*

Having been advanced to the front line of wine topics, wine-food combination is now viewed with utmost seriousness of purpose by many would-be gastronomes. In some circles a perceived *faux pas* may be construed as a lack of respect for either the wine or the food, or else for one's guests, and this brings with it one of life's minor but no less felt social humiliations. The potential for embarrassment has provided the quicksand for the rooting of several 'schools' of wine-food combination, whose advices are intended, at the least, to avert gustative disaster, if not actually to ensure palatal nirvana on each and every occasion. Five such schools are in vogue, and they represent two eras, as follows.

OLD WORLD ERA. The first three schools originated before the Second World War among traditionalist connoisseurs who saw wine geographically as being limited to the familiar West European regions.

Metaphysical Rightness

The oldest of the formal schools, this one dates to late-19th century connoisseurs who assumed that the goodness of a combination proceeds from the intrinsic suitability of it. Such suitability typically was reckoned by reference to 'congruent prestige,' whereby wines of first-rank quality *ipso facto* could only be suited to pairing with dishes of first-rank quality; and theoretically, so it went down the gastronomic hierarchy, except that in practice the founding enophiles of *Metaphysical Rightness* did not deign to combine below second-rank quality. The lack of post-mortem critical commentary on the combinations in the gastronomic literature of the day suggests that the very names of the dishes and wines seen on extant menus were presumed to be sufficient proof of the validity of the pairings.

Concerning Clarret & Botargo

Although a few practitioners of the congruent prestige stripe persist today, most latter-day adherents of *Metaphysical Rightness* do expect to be convinced by actual gustative complementariness between the partners – however complementariness be understood. The old guard and the vanguard agree chiefly in the inclination to derive rankings for unfamiliar wine types from the established rankings of familiar foods that are judged to be the most suitable complements (for example, a varietally odd or geographically strange wine that suits Yankee Pot Roast to a tee will never be considered higher than third-rank quality).

National Parallelism

In an era dominated by the nation-state it was perhaps inevitable that it would occur to some enophiles of the late 19th and early 20th centuries that a special, qualitatively inimitable relationship exists between the wines and foods of individual wine producing countries. This school owed its beginnings to peripatetic European enophile eccentrics in the early period of the *service à la Russe*, who intuited that each nation's cooks and wine makers had cooperated for centuries, if only tacitly, to bring out complementary flavors in their characteristic dishes and wines. But this perspective only gained real momentum because of its utility to mainstream *Metaphysical Rightness* believers when they found themselves abroad, exposed to wines they were unfamiliar with, especially when they presumed them to rank below second quality.

In the post-Second World War decades, the ranks of *National Parallelism* followers burgeoned with the explosion of travel on the European continent, and more recently with the school's adaptability to downsizing from the nation-state to the regional and/or ethnic level (Catalan style vs. Spanish style, etc.). But historically oriented extremists are loathe to pair post-Columbian European national/regional/ethnic dishes with pre-Columbian wine types, which grates on moderates who, for instance, habitually accompany neo-Italian tomato sauce with red varietals of Greco-Roman or Etruscan extraction. Meanwhile, the future serviceability of *National Parallelism* has been cast into doubt by the global spread of fusion cuisine.

Desert Island Wine

Territorial Propinquity

This school began as an offshoot of *National Parallelism* among gourmets of the interwar period of the 20th century, who as a result of sojourns or repeated visits in particular locales known for an array of typical local foodstuffs, dishes and beverages, concluded that a natural, 'organic' affinity exists between the food and drink of restricted locales, such that the environment – virtually independently of anything done by cooks and wine makers or bakers and brewers – confers on its products a tendency towards mutually supportive flavor resonance in the mouth. This resonance is attributed either to like strains of flavor, such as 'smokiness' caused by volcanic soil, or more fundamentally, to shared compositional elements, such as traces of minerals x, y and z, etc.

Territorial Propinquity gained notable popularity beginning in the 1980s as a result of heightened verbiage about *terroir* in wine literature read at home, reinforced by the self-fulfilling prophecy syndrome engaged by the imagination when enophiles found themselves on-site. Conversely, this school's potential spread has been held back by stay-at-home enophiles who are more attracted by guidance on what is available in the neighborhood.

NEW AGE ERA. The other two schools developed primarily in the New World, as a result of the expanding geography of 'fine wine' after the Second World War.

Intensity Harmonization

Offering something like a 'decibel' approach to combinations, the fundamental precept of this school is that the relative flavor intensity of a food or wine demands a partner of analogous intensity (that is, bold with bold; unaccented with unaccented, etc.). It is actually the oldest of practical notions as to what wines and what foods are to be consumed together, since its origin is in the age-old practical Mediterranean habit of drinking light (usually white or rosé) wines in warm weather, when salads, vegetables and fish are plentiful, and heavy (usually red) wines in cold weather, when animal fats and gamy meats are sought.

But as a formal school, *Intensity Harmonization* dates only to the 1970s. It arose mainly because of the difficulty of credibly accommodating the earlier theories of wine-food combination to New World wines (for instance, the specific American dilemma of what to do at dinner with big zinfandel wines). But the school has spread further in tandem with the export of those wines to the Old World, as well as the migration of non-European cuisines (for instance, the British dilemma of what to drink in London with Indian cuisine).

This school almost invariably is the first beneficiary from the food trends that come along in today's cross-cultural context, whether the trend is ingredient-based (for example, tofu) or style-based (for example, 'blackened' anything).

Scientific Determinism

The rising importance of combinations in New World wine journals of the late 1970s spawned an intensely earnest type of enophile who, in the search for greater certainty of results, turned to science. Specifically this meant the exploration of chemical interactions, which are viewed as unfailing in their operation and knowable in their effects on the human sensory apparatus. On the practical side this school insists that by adhering to chemically guided pairings, any knowledgeable cook or cellar-person will be able to equal or surpass the goodness of any wine-food combination achieved impersonally by a micro-environment (in an earlier time these believers would have adhered to the *Territorial Propinquity* school).

This school appeals especially to New World enophiles and gourmets who sense that their native wines and foods lack standing because of insufficient *terroir* development, and can only be vindicated and respected internationally through combinations that are second to none. But an *avant-garde* segment of neuro-chemically oriented European Greens also is attracted to Scientific Determinism. The school is especially preoccupied with compiling the 'natural laws' that govern combining ("it's a matter of chemistry, not opinion"), a task ultimately to be justified and rewarded by a comprehensive list of sanctioned and proscribed chemical interactions.

But while each of the five schools has its enthusiasts, some enophiles do not treat the several concepts as mutually exclusive, but instead draw upon all of them as the occasion suggests. It is even possible that behind closed doors the publicly disavowed old rule of thumb, 'red wine with red meats, white wine with white meats and fish,' hangs on in daily practice, albeit with greater sensitivity to shifts in food ideology.

*

The benefit to wine appreciation from the recent fascination with combinations is unclear. While greater sensual gratification is a self-apparent goal of everything written on the subject, evidence of genuine intellectual fruit is scanty. Wine-food combination has yet to result, for instance, in an enlightened reassessment of the various kinds and styles of wines in the light of their broader gastronomic merits.

Further, enophiles may be referencing the several concepts of combination chiefly to lift from their faculties the burden of interpreting what their senses might otherwise perceive, in the way the philosopher Bergson meant when he wrote that by actually paying attention to a taste you might find out that you do not like it as much as you thought you would. Overall, therefore, today's enophiles may be little ahead mentally, while lagging considerably in morale, compared to the forebears from whom they have inherited so many of the wines and foods being combined.

*

"After dinner to the office, where we stayed and did business; and then Sir W. Penn and I went home with Sir R. Slingsby to bowles in his ally and there had good sport; and afterward went in and drank and talked. So home, Sir William and I; and it being very hot weather, I took my flagilette and played upon the leads in the garden, where Sir W. Penn came out in his shirt into his leads and there we stayed drinking great draughts of Clarret and eating botargo and bread and butter till 12 at night, it being moonshine. And so to bed – very near fuddled."

Samuel Pepys,
Diary, 4-6 June, 1661

*   *   *

From our compendium of X-rated wine-food combinations.

19

MED FLY

The olive-based Mediterranean diet has not changed much since Hippocrates wrote *Regimen*. But these days the northern European meat-and-potatoes regime is giving the Father of Medicine a run for the money on his home turf, and a fast-food hamburger may just as likely be encountered as *mousaka*. Of course, though, some enophiles do not acknowledge much difference between hamburger and *mousaka* as regards wine-food combinations. This calls for a closer examination of olive oil and *mousaka*, specifically the kind based on eggplant.

The contemporary enophile certainly cannot afford to gloss over olive oil now that The Mediterranean Diet is being widely embraced. As the ancients pointed out, olive oil's perfectly round particles press aromas to gather and mingle closely, so as to produce a more unified and persistent smell and flavor in the finished dish. Olive oil dishes thus fill in flavor gaps in plain wine and invite it to the table more frequently than butter has done. But there's the rub for the future of wine appreciation in this new alimentary era: Olive oil is ambiguous in its social moorings and can be the most democratic of fats.

But there is no ambiguity about a noble *mousaka*. A proper one is an olive oil dish par excellence. Its most constant constituent over time and space has been eggplant, indeed the true protagonist in the genesis of *mousaka*. Eggplant's affinity for olive oil is as celebrated in the East as it has been notorious in the West, and this fact is central to *mousaka*'s combination with wine.

Olive oil puddles are natural to *mousaka*. Aficionados advise taking to them with bread even before piercing the custard cap with a fork. In its puddles may be read the entire history of a *mousaka*. As this history can span upwards of a week, the reward is great. It is no small irony that now, just when olive oil is waxing, a movement is underway among some less unctuous chefs to see to the mopping up of the puddles before the plate ever reaches the table, or even to forestall a drip by eschewing extravagance in the early stages of assembling eggplant *mousaka*.

But the exact classification of *mousaka* is a bit of a head-scratcher and probably depends mostly on how one can best slice it. *Mousaka* certainly cannot lay with the *en croûte* delicacies; but on the other hand it does not sink with the fluid casseroles, either. Sometimes it seems to slide in between the *terrines* and *pâtés*: it leans towards *terrines* if it is of the high-built kind and served at Mediterranean room temperature when several days old; and towards *pâtés* if it is also crusty and baked with a lining of eggplant skins. However, the rarer low-built *mousaka*, with its slim strata, cuts nicely on the bias and, if highly flavored with sweet spices, can for all the world seem a soft, non-stick *baklava* that does not necessarily defy pairing with a sweet wine.

The familiar custard cap is a mark of *O Megas Mousakas* (*Le Grand Mousaka*). This superstructure also undergirds those who maintain that *mousaka* could reflect elements of Byzantine cuisine that were preserved by monastic communities and the wealthy classes. White sauce after all was invented by the ancient Greeks; and the possession of such lush skills is only reinforced by an early 19th century notation that "the *blanc manger* [sic], in Greek *thiason*, is not much known [in the Balkans] outside the refined Greek kitchen."

This is not to intimate that Hippocrates would recognize *mousaka*. But neither is a classical lineage out of the question. For in addition to white sauce the ancient Greeks also knew the frying pan, ground meat and sweet spices. What is more, according to one of Plutarch's dining companions (in *Table-talk*), the ancient Greeks had become rather undemocratically clever at concocting sloppy dishes:

> "The custom of distributing portions of meat was abandoned
> when dinners became extravagant; for it was not possible, I
> suppose, to divide fancy cakes and Lydian puddings and rich
> sauces and all sorts of other dishes made of ground and grated
> delicacies; these luxurious dainties got the better of men and the
> custom of an equal share for all was abandoned."

In none of its manifestations is *mousaka* a finger-food.

Med Fly

For the bibulous diner all other issues necessarily drown in the question of which wine to drink with *mousaka*. The simplest solution is the one blandly offered by The Great Connoisseurs of wine, who remain under the influence of olive oil's old association with swarthy populations lacking in pedigree and given to swilling oxidized white wines and *corsé* reds. These commentators lump *mousaka* with The Great Meatloafs and assign it to the lower middle rank of dishes, and advise drinking with it either resinated white wines or third-rate wines of color, in either case to chase the olive oil. But this view, mired as it is in a lack of the Classical wisdom about olive oil's contribution to aromatic savor, fails alike the friend of wine and the friend of *mousaka*. At the very least, a Hippocratic approach to prescriptions for the combination of *mousaka* and wine is in order:

Now, fresh baked *mousaka* has not geled in either consistency or flavor and should be followed by young wines of mild flavor served cool; conversely, half-baked connoisseurs must at all costs avoid aged red wines and overheating themselves. *Mousaka* is most easily digested when it is 2- or 3-days-old, at which time soft and aromatic white wines at cool-room temperature are to be recommended; but once mellowing is noticed in the imbiber, further quaffing should be curtailed lest the beneficial effects of this treatment be ground down. The gastronomic potential of *mousaka* generally peaks at 3 to 5 days, at which point fat wines are exercised in their aromatic properties and middle-aged diners will sit still and gush; however, if reheated more than twice, *mousaka* can suffer oven stress and acquire a smoky by-taste that calls for either tannic young red wine or oxidized white wine in order to suppress sympathetically morbid reactions in the diner. *Mousaka* either 1-day-old and cool or more than 5-days-old and warm needs only plain wine.

*   *   *

He told me…that mine was the middle state, or what might be called the upper station of low life, which he had found by long experience was the best state in the world, not exposed to the miseries and hardships, the labor and sufferings of the mechanic part of mankind and not embarrassed with the pride, luxury, ambition, and envy of the upper part.

Daniel Defoe,
Robinson Crusoe, 1719

20

EPAULET, PALETTE, PALATE

Anyone who is entertaining thoughts of getting serious about wine would do themselves a huge favor by first checking their lineage to see if they have what it takes. Our genes do not prepare all of us equally for this art. I discovered much too late, after for years having sunk inexcusably substantial portions of my annual disposable income into the upkeep of vineyard estates where I would never be deemed a fit tasting companion, that my family tree was planted in the wrong soil for appreciation of the finest wines to take root in me. I gave up the hope of uncovering anything but yeoman ancestors after reaching documentation from four generations and a century-and-a-half back, and with that, also the illusion that any of them could have known how to do anything with wine besides gulp it. The closest that any blood relative came to rising above the family's congenital station was when one became a salaried employee on an estate of Count Barkóczy in Upper Hungary, but that's only in line with where I stand in Winedom today.

Palatal elitism rooted itself in the firmament of gastronomic tradition at an early date. Already by the 1st century A.D., Plutarch (*Table-talk*) must have felt there was more than ample reason to speak out against the excesses:

> If in other matters we are to preserve equality among men, why not begin with the first and accustom them to take their places with each other without vanity and ostentation, because they

understand as soon as they enter the door that the dinner is a democratic affair and has no outstanding place like an acropolis where the rich man is to recline and lord it over the meaner folk?

Nevertheless, the protagonists of all that is noble in food and drink went merrily on their way and perpetrated a caste system of the mouth. Their subtle message – that it is good and right for people to enjoy fine wine so long as they are not The People – echoed through the centuries and penetrated the thick skull of the masses, who now resolutely avoid the labels they can see are not meant for display at their hearth – if their betters have not already seen to making that clear on the invoice. Lost to the fabled generosity of enophiles is the ancient Greek conception of Dionysus as "the original ploughman" (Plutarch), an agrarian and egalitarian god.

But wine growing practices may themselves have been a source of palatal 'standing.' In ancient Mediterranean agriculture vines often were trained up trees, so that harvesters had to go up after the fruit. Evidence from the parallel case of olive harvesters on the Greek island of Zakynthos suggests that a kind of hierarchical jargon could have developed to designate the relative positions of the grape-gatherers. By age-old habit the Zakynthian olive harvesters are classed either as 'uppers' or 'lowers' according to whether they are stationed, respectively, standing high among the branches or kneeling down on the ground. Further, such classing may have been based on physical or social factors having nothing to do with the work as such. For instance, the Zakynthians make their division by gender, with the males always the uppers and the females always the lowers. But viticulture is tainted from an early date in any case because of Cato's advice, "Gather the inferior grapes for the sharp wine for the hands to drink."

What we are confronting is the bottomless hole known to philosophers as 'the genetic fallacy.' As the name suggests, birth and origins are at issue, although it may also extend to physical traits. Practical justifications occasionally may weigh in, as when the Zakynthians explain their use of the natural hierarchy in olive harvesting by pointing out that few olives would be collected if the skirted females were to become uppers. However, in its more advanced manifestations the genetic fallacy comes into play when we try to make heads or tails of a thing's present nature by reference to something in its origin or development even though it is something several times removed from the thing itself, and quite incidental to it. It was by resort to the genetic fallacy that Columella (*De Re Rustica*) hoped to ensure quality in grapes and wine:

> Vineyards require not so much tall men as those who are
> broad-shouldered and brawny, for this type is better suited
> to digging and pruning and other forms of viticulture.

Taking Columella to the logical conclusion, we should have to size up Château X's vineyard help just in case the property might need to be reclassified.

These days we are plied with 'genetic' information of various kinds about wine. But no such instances fire the consumer spirit and imagination quite as much as those which encourage us to derive a qualitative impression of a wine from what we know of the genesis of the producer, or more specifically, the producer's social origin or status. We have a predilection to imagine the maker of 'aristocratic' wine as necessarily having a claim, however tenuous, on aristocracy of one kind or another. Certainly our ego is gently massaged by sketches of stately dwellings on labels, which suggest that for the indicated price – really a modest one in almost any case for what it is we want – we lowers may briefly climb out of our pit to lift the skirts of the uppers.

The measure used is usually the time-honored one of nobility and bloodline. Under its influence we do such things as attribute greater quality to a wine produced by someone who is, say, a wealthy art dealer and polo-player whose family belonged to the nobility (whether greater or lesser). But sometimes we revamp the idea along republican lines by identifying wealth as the prerequisite for the production of outstanding wine, as though we should obtain the producer's financial statement before investing in a wooden crate of pricey bottles. But in either case, nobility or liquidity, we are expecting that 'pedigree,' 'breed,' 'class' and 'distinction' in the person must somehow transfer to the wine. It should be no surprise that the words of praise for both the persons and their wines tend to be exactly the same.

The seed for our talk of vinous heraldry was sown around the early 4th century B.C. It is possible to specify this period because when Plato in that century used the word *gennaios* to indicate 'choice' grapes and figs, he qualified it with the expression "now called," thereby indicating a new conception that must have entered speech only during his lifetime.

Epaulet, Palette, Palate

Gennaios has the same root as 'genesis,' and Athenaeus (*The Deipnosophists*) said that Plato had meant it as 'well-born' or 'high-bred.' (In modern Greek the term corresponds to 'generous' and 'chivalrous,' while the related term *eugenis* corresponds to 'noble' and 'polite.') But ancient authors rarely invoked the concept of nobility when writing about agriculture or gastronomy. Plutarch said that 'noble crops' (*gennaious karpous*) might be had even from difficult land if care were taken; Columella said that some types of vines achieve 'nobility' (*nobilitantur*) if their grapes are harvested and their wines made properly; he also cited advice on planting 'superior vines' (*nobilem vitem*); and Athenaeus called one wine *eugenis* without suggesting its superiority over numerous others that he praised with other words. The shared contextual meaning in these instances seems to have been no more – but no less, either – than the now outclassed 'excellent.' Indeed, after his mention of 'nobility' in vine types, Columella immediately went on to say that "almost every wine has the property of acquiring *excellence* with age" (emphasis added). But 'excellent' was also the word used by the translator Lefebvre de Villebrune in the 1780s in rendering Athenaeus's term *eugenis* in French in the cited instance. For that matter, the early Greek expression *aristos oinos* did not mean 'aristocratic wine' as we would invoke it, but only 'excellent wine.'

Did the revolutionary, republican passion for social justice in France in de Villebrune's day dictate his circumspection in avoiding 'noble'? Perhaps. The word apparently had already started slipping off tongues and pens in western Europe by that time, since by 1796 it had made its way to America, where Amelia Simmons, in her *American Cookery* of that year, referred to perch and roach as "noble pan fish" and called salmon "the noblest and richest fish." Yet even in 1816, when a French writer might have taken more liberties, André Jullien made no mention of 'noble' as a wine term in *Topographie de Tous Les Vignobles Connus*. Nor did writers on wine in the late 19th century render any fealty to concepts like 'noble varieties.' Anglophone writers became enamored of 'aristocratic' wines only during the first part of the 20th century.

The modern impetus for injecting nobility into wine appreciation may have come from further east, from Upper Hungary, the source of 'Imperial Tokay.' One of the earliest modern books in which the word noble recurs is one written in Latin about Tokaji by the Hungarian Antal Szirmay in 1798. Aristocratic producers of Tokaji who saw to it that those of their kind elsewhere in Europe were treated to their wine must also have been sure to let the recipients know just which words to apply. Ironically, Hungarians of the 19th century were so effectively able to use the aura of the Habsburgs in selling the West on 'Imperial Tokay' that the verbal associations eventually backfired on them after the First World War and the collapse of the monarchy:

> ...Tokay, which itself will probably never recover the disappearance of those Hapsburgs, with whom it was so inseparably connected. Republican Tokay would be a contradiction in terms. But to tell the truth, it never was a wine: only a prince of liqueurs.

(George Saintsbury, *Notes on a Cellar-Book*, 1920)

The prince-and-pauper reading of wines was further encouraged by the premise that a bottle of wine can have the same attributes as an *objet d'art*. This view ascribed to bottled wines the function of museum pieces that retain their aesthetic merit beyond the generation that witnessed the creation of the object, hence the phenomenon of wine as a collectible per se. Because artistic beauty of that sort historically reached apogees by the grace of lordly patrons, such a personage is taken to be a condition, not just a circumstance, of the esteemed sensory experience. The portrayal of wine making as a 'fine art' is so commonplace nowadays that wine makers are accorded the status of 'artist' without the least reservation ("the sparkling wine was Prosecco di Conegliano *by* Carpenè Malvolti" – emphasis added).

But the position of wine making as an art is wobbly. The problem is that its result, wine, is an article for bodily ingestion, destined by its nature to be used, willy-nilly, for its nutritive value by our physical self. Consequently, unlike a poem or painting or other product of the true arts, a wine is only in part susceptible of aesthetic appreciation in the way of an honest subjective regard for outward qualities such as appearance, smell and flavor. Another part, namely the wine's inner substance that constitutes its nourishing properties, lies beyond that possibility and must be assimilated to our body before we can grasp the wine for all that it essentially is.

Further, this involuntary corporeal 'appreciation' is objective in that we cannot influence the body's use of the wine's stuff even if to some hazy extent we may be conscious of a few of our specific physiological reactions.

Epaulet, Palette, Palate

Thus, each wine, although created through selected manipulations of wine making, possesses an intrinsic value that cannot be augmented by the 'creativity' of the wine maker. Instead, the comparative worth of an individual wine as a comestible can only *seem* to be inflated through hype and cajolery that spur our ego to find heightened satisfaction. It was because psycho-emotional gratification takes precedence over intellect in our response to the results of cookery, that Socrates denied the status of art to cuisine:

> Socrates: Ask me, then, what sort of an art in my opinion, is cookery?
>
> Polus: All right, I'm asking. What art is cookery?
>
> Socrates: None at all, Polus.
>
> Polus: Then what is it? Tell me.
>
> Socrates: I say that it is a certain knack.
>
> Polus: A knack of what, if you please?
>
> Socrates: I say a knack of producing gratification and pleasure, Polus.
>
> Polus: So cooking and rhetoric are the same thing?
>
> Socrates: Not at all; both are branches of the same pursuit...which has nothing 'fine' about it at all...and seems not to be an artistic pursuit at all, but that of a shrewd, courageous spirit which is naturally clever at dealing with men; and I call the chief part of it flattery. It seems to me to have many branches and one of them is cookery, which is thought to be an art, but according to my notion is no art at all, but a knack and a routine. I hold that rhetoric, too, is a branch of this pursuit, and so is make-up and sophistic – four branches applied to four different things.

(Plato, *Gorgias*)

Desert Island Wine

From the Socratic viewpoint, wine makers, through practice and talent in bringing forth a wholesome comestible, merit the less furbeloved title of artisan: "What is an artisan? one who knows how to produce something useful?" (Socrates, in Xenophon's *Memorabilia*). An implication of this status as a craft, rather than as an art, is that nothing about wine making can be construed as having an intrinsic feature that necessarily makes it more susceptible of conscientious and successful elaboration by the few than by hoi polloi. Modern science obscured this in the 19th century and the early 20th century, when its information, having become a chief element of carefulness, was also nearly the exclusive preserve of the privileged and literate classes. But by a remarkable turn of events, republican principles enabled the spread of public education and put the new practical knowledge at the disposal of all. As a result, it is no longer necessary for socially obscure and financially marginal wine makers to throw in the towel early.

Xenophon, in *The Oeconomicus*, related Socrates's questioning of the gentleman farmer Ischomachus. Socrates was probing the relationship of 'good,' in the sense of 'worthy,' to 'beautiful.' The philosopher was troubled that the two words were blended in the term *kagathos*, which meant 'gentleman,' and he wondered what justified their joining. Having never belonged to the right drinking society – we all know what a fine vintage was finally poured for Socrates by the worthy gentlemen of Athens – the old gadfly found no necessary relationship at all, and at length he drew out of Ischomachus that diligence, and no other personal attribute, was the key to success in the georgic crafts:

> "Well, Socrates, you shall now hear how kindly is this art of agriculture. Helpful, pleasant, honourable, dear to gods and men in the highest degree, it is also in the highest degree easy to learn. Noble qualities surely."

* * *

21

Karaghiozis is the central character of Greek shadow puppet theatre. His schemes to escape poverty without much effort are endless; his cunning is represented by an exceedingly long and flexible arm. Though rooted in Ottoman times, he is always at home in the contemporary scene. He is cast here as…

KARAGHIOZIS, WINE MAKER EXTRAORDINAIRE

Characters:

Karaghiozis
Hadjiavatis, a villager
Stavrakas, a villager
Sultan
Hassan Aga, aide to the Sultan,
Sior Dionyius, a gentleman of Corfu
Mrs. Karaghiozis

ACT I

Scene: Karaghiozis's dilapidated hut. In front, tables with umbrellas and chairs. Signs on the wall read 'Extra Virgin Wine,' 'All Appellations' 'EUROs Accepted.' No one is present.

(Enter Hadjiavatis wearing garlands of garlic)

Hadjiavatis: Karaghiozis! Where are you? I can't even find your door for all these tables and chairs. What the devil is going on?

Karaghiozis: *(unseen)* I'm down here in the cellar – where a great artist belongs.

Hadjiavatis: Artist, you say? When did you start painting? Are you going to whitewash this place?

Karaghiozis: Paint, schmaint. I'm a wine maker. No brushes for me. But a palate comes in handy. And a wine-thief just to keep things honest.

Desert Island Wine

Hadjiavatis: Turning to thieving, are you? Need to steal some grapes, do you?

Karaghiozis: We're talking about wine, not grapes! Anybody with half a brain and two-thirds of a birthright could make wine from grapes. Do I look like an Antinori? a Mondavi? a Boutari, even?

Hadjiavatis: You just look like Karaghiozis to me, so I thought you needed – what do they call it? – 'raw materials.' You know, grapes.

Karaghiozis: 'Raw materials' is one thing. But grapes are beneath me. (And any that find their way into this hut are going to go into our bellies just as they are.) This here is artistry and sophistication. It's what wine lovers pay for.

Hadjiavatis: So, the missus finally forced you to get a job. Is it time for that wine festival at Dafni again? And the National Tourist Organization has given you a post?

Karaghiozis: Dafni?! Hmmph! Dafni just goes to show that grapes don't have to give wine – all those tourists guzzling belly-wash that the European Union wouldn't even buy to make into rubbing alcohol. Instead of dancing and smashing plates at Dafni, somebody ought to be cracking skulls at the National Tourist Organization. It's a national disgrace, is what it is. I'm a supra-nationalist and above all that. Oh, for a respectable Vinexpo. Then I'd show'em a thing or two.

Hadjiavatis: European Union? Aren't they the ones who pay me to bury my peaches in the ground every year? No wonder you're all worked up. I guess you'll fix them, huh? Can I come down and see history in the making?

Karaghiozis: If you take so much as one step down I'll box your ears for you, you bundle of barrel staves. Bacchus only knows who you'd go blabbing to. Did Rommel map out campaigns with Montgomery looking over his shoulder? Did Mozart compose with Salieri in earshot? Does Troigros … Oh, now you've done it! You've made one wan man go and think of Troisgros. It sets my mouth to watering. All those dishes and stars. But this hovel never sees anything grander than bean stew. And its master an artist!

Karaghiozis, Wine Maker Extraordinaire

(Karaghiozis emerges from the cellar and boxes Hadjiavatis's ears)

Hadjiavatis: Have mercy, Karaghiozis!   It's me who's always giving Madame Karaghiozis the garlic for your bean stew.   Where would wine be if it weren't for garlic?

Karaghiozis: Yes, and I've half a mind to throw you down stairs just to wipe out my stinking debt.   But then you'd learn my secrets.   Be gone! You're giving me heartburn on an empty stomach.   And take your garlic with you, lest it befoul the wine the way it does my mouth.

ACT II

Scene: Roadside tavern. Stavrakas is seated at a table with a pitcher and a glass.

(Enter Hadjiavatis)

Stavrakas: Yo-ho, Hadjiavatis!   Come join me and have a glass of wine. This is the best stuff around, let me tell you.   Thank goodness those wine journalists don't know about it.   The tourists would be on this place like flies.

Hadjiavatis: Please, I don't want to hear about wine.   I've just come from Karaghiozis's and wine's a sore point with me.

Stavrakas: What's he up to now?   A new scheme?

Hadjiavatis: Says he's an artist.   But all he's doing is making some secret kind of wine for some club of xenophobes or some such in Europe.

Stavrakas: Artist?   If he wants to dabble, he ought to at least become an amateur.   He sure could learn a thing or two from this wine.

Hadjiavatis: Well, I wouldn't sit here with him if I were you.   I think wine's gone to his head already, if you ask me.   But maybe he'll tell you how someone without grapes can make wine.   He won't tell me, and I sure can't figure it out.

Desert Island Wine

Stavrakas: *(scratches his head a few moments)* Aha! I heard the Sultan has announced a standing offer of a handsome prize to his first subject who succeeds in making wine that isn't wine. He would give anything to savor the taste of wine, but his holy book won't hear of it and the only way out is a drink that passes for wine but isn't wine.

Hadjiavatis: Wine that isn't wine? What will it be then?

Stavrakas: Better you find out from Karaghiozis. As for me, I'll stick with what nature has provided here.

ACT III

Scene: The Sultan's chambers. Empty boxes of Turkish delight lay scattered about in all directions. The Sultan and Sior Dionysius are present.

Sior Dionysius: Mighty Master of the Sweetmeats! A new shipment of Turkish delight has arrived from your favorite confectioner's. Shall I have it brought in?

Sultan: *(paging through the Koran)* Just what I need! More Turkish delight! It is going to be the end of me – to say nothing of my dentures. Oh, if only I had some wine to chew on. You'd think that with all these Fundamentalists running around this blasted realm at least one could get down to basics and figure out wine so I could have wine that isn't wine and stop yearning for the real thing. Just look at me, spending my days searching through this book for an escape clause. What's the use of being a sultan if I have to die and go to heaven to have wine, while all my infidel subjects get to taste heaven right here on earth?

Sior Dionysius: Maybe if we steep the Turkish delight in vinegar it will give a close approximation. Once on Corfu, I …

Sultan: Wine out of Turkish delight?! Better a mash be made out of you, winy as you are.

Sior Dionysius: Then how about we bring in some of those biotechnologists from abroad? If they can make genetically modified soybeans, they can probably come up with genetically modified wine too.

Karaghiozis, Wine Maker Extraordinaire

Sultan: At last you're putting those Ionian noodles to work. Let's call in the Australians. Or is it the Americans? I can never remember who does what when it comes to wine.

(Enter Hassan Aga)

Hassan Aga: Wait! Don't call in anybody. I bring great tidings, Most Sublime Ex-Teetotaler. Word comes that our very own Karaghiozis has invented wine that isn't wine. He has invited you to his cellar for a tasting.

Sultan: *(tossing the Koran onto some empty boxes of Turkish delight)* What are we waiting for, then? Let us be off to see him at once. I should have known I could count on my faithful subject, Karaghiozis.

ACT IV

Scene: Karaghiozis's cellar. Karaghiozis sits pouring from vials into various beakers marked Bordeaux, Burgundy, Port and Local Stuff. To the rear are shelves lined with jars marked Prune Juice, Herbes de Provence, Liquid Smoke, Maple Syrup, Worcesterhire Sauce, etc.

(A knock is heard on the cellar door)

Karaghiozis: Get away, Hadjiavatis! I've no time for you. Wine may wait, but not wine that is not wine.

Sultan: Karaghiozis! It is me, the Sultan. Is it true, my son, that you have uncorked the secrets of wine and are going to deliver me from my tedious existence? But do open up and let us come down for a trial.

(Karaghiozis opens the door and the Sultan, Hassan Aga and Sior Dionysius troop down)

Karaghiozis: Most Exalted Connoisseur of Finer Things! I have indeed unraveled all there is to know about wine and tied it all back together again so as to be wine without being wine. Just feast your eyes on these humble labels! What is your preference? Bordeaux? Burgundy? Port? You name it, I have it – or can very soon.

Desert Island Wine

Hassan Aga: *(whispering urgently to the Sultan)* The Bordeaux! Take the Bordeaux!

Sultan: *(to Hassan Aga)* What do you know about it? Let Sior Dionysius here pick and taste and pronounce.

Hassan Aga: Why, he's no more than a tippler of Ionian currant juice. I've read dozens of wine books from my annual pilgrimages to Harrod's.

Sultan: But have you not been clutching the same holy book as me? Or have you been taking off your fez when they come by with the beverage cart on British Air? And besides, what is there about wine that isn't wine that a nobleman wouldn't know? No, it must be Sior Dionysius.

Karaghiozis: That settles it then. *(handing a glass to Sior Dionysius)* Here, take this glass and order up. What'll it be?

Sior Dionysius: Do you have any Ionian kinds? I'd love to drink something worthy of Corfu. Ever since the days when …

Karaghiozis: *(pulling Sior Dionysius towards him by the collar)* Listen, you meatball, if you go making any trouble for me, I'll tan your hide so hard you'll swear these are the softest tannins you've ever tasted.

Sior Dionysius: *(released by Karaghiozis)* On second thought, let it be the Bordeaux. Every enophile with a mind of his own knows that's the way to go.

(Karaghiozis pours. Sior Dionysius sniffs at the glass. Karaghiozis pushes his face into it.)

Karaghiozis: We don't have all day! Get on with it! No looking gift horses in the nose. My wines are honest and you can taste everything you smell.

Sior Dionysius: *(after tasting)* Yes! Yes! Médoc. No, wait a second. Actually, Napa, I think. Aha! Rutherford Bench. Oh, do let me sit down. I ponder these things so much better when I'm anchored.

Karaghiozis, Wine Maker Extraordinaire

(Karaghiozis shoves a chair behind Sior Dionysius, who drops onto it)

Karaghiozis: *(thinking aloud)* Hmm, I'd better go lighter on the mint with the next Bordeaux batch.

(Hassan Aga tries to reach for the glass, but the Sultan catches his hand and empties the glass onto the floor)

Hassan Aga: Let's move on to the Burgundy: the Wine of Sultans and the Sultan of Wines!

(Karaghiozis pours from the flask marked 'Burgundy')

Sior Dionysius: *(after tasting)* Sort of velvety. No, no. Felt. That's it, felt all the way down.

Hassan Aga: *(whispering to the Sultan)* It's supposed to be velvet and not felt.

Sultan: *(shouting back)* No! It's supposed to be wine that is not wine, is all.

Karaghiozis: *(thinking aloud)* Hmm, a bigger dose of sultana essence for my Burgundy next time around. *(shrugging)* They've done worse in Beaune, heaven knows.

Sultan: Well, on to the next one. The Port – or is it Porte? Ha, ha, ha! A sultan in every Porte and a Port in every sultan. Ha, Ha, Ha! I am feeling giddy already.

(Karaghiozis pours the 'Port')

Sior Dionysius: *(takes a taste and shoots back from the table, gasping)* Water, somebody! Quick! *(Karaghiozis draws from a barrel marked 'Futuristic Wine' and pours it over Sior Dionysius)* A refreshing finish, but a hellish start. More of an assault than an attack, I'd say.

Desert Island Wine

Karaghiozis: *(anxiously)* Well, what more proof do you need? It obviously smacks of wine. *(thinking aloud)* I'll have to cut back to steeping the chilies only 10 minutes for my next Port, or else replace the serranos with jalapeños. Oh! my head is aching – wine is such a calculating art.

Hassan Aga: But there's still the Local Stuff. We can't very well have done with it without trying what we – I mean, you – know best.

(Karaghiozis pours the 'Local Stuff')

Sior Dionysius: *(takes a swig and spits it out at once in a blast)* He's got it down pat there.

Sultan: Bravo, Karaghiozis! Bravissimo! Well, don't just stand there, my boy. Pour me some. The Bordeaux. No, the Burgundy. No, the Port. No, the Local Stuff. Oh, drat. I am free as a bird at last, but I don't know how to fly.

Karaghiozis: Let me recommend a cocktail from them all, Your Most Exalted Palateship.

Sultan: Yes! Of course! It'll be like one of those wine tastings I've heard about, except I'll do it all at one go and have all the benefits at once. *(Karaghiozis pours from the several beakers and hands the glass to the Sultan, who takes a mouthful)* Oh, but it is exquisite. It is like kumquat. No, almonds. No, rose water. No, sesame. No ... but what's the point of going on with my poor descriptions? By Allah, you've done it, Karaghiozis, Lord of the Casks. *(to Sior Dionysius)* Have that last shipment of Turkish delight returned. I won't be needing it.

Sior Dionysius: May I keep the refund?

Sultan: What you may keep is your mouth shut, especially around this marvelous potation, lest I send you packing for the ferry to Corfu. *(to Karaghiozis)* Your genius is testament to the wisdom of keeping my subjects on their bare toes. You will be made Imperial Supplier of Wine-That-Is-Not-Wine, and you will enjoy exclusive sales rights throughout the realm.

Karaghiozis, Wine Maker Extraordinaire

ACT V

Scene: Outside Karaghiozis's hut. Sign on the door reads, 'Temporarily Closed – Proprietor Abroad.' Several crates marked 'WINE-THAT-IS-NOT-WINE' and 'Handle With More Than Your Usual Care' are stacked up. Karaghiozis and Hadjiavatis are present.

Hadjiavatis: How many bundles are you taking, Karaghiozis? You'll keep the Customs people busy for hours.

Karaghiozis: What Customs? We're in the European Union and I'm a wine maker without borders. And it's not everyday I'm called to Brussels.

Hadjiavatis: What? Brussels? Sprouts?

Karaghiozis: Don't you even think Brussels Sprouts around my wines!! – you'll ruin the aftertaste. No, Brussels, Belgium, you cabbage head. It's where the European Union hangs out, and they've summoned me to drain the Wine Lake. They want to fund me to expand my cellar so I can halt the wine overflow.

Hadjiavatis: Wine Lake? Overflow? So, how come I'm not swimming in wine?

Karaghiozis: You're lucky you have water to tread. Look, there are too many vineyards over in Europe and my Wine-That-Is-Not-Wine means there will never be too much wine ... or too little, either. Supply and demand will always balance.

Hadjiavatis: I wish you would talk plainly and leave all the rest to the folks in Sprouts. It's all over my head, Karaghiozis, ol' pip.

Karaghiozis: The only head of yours that concerns me is garlic. This is my chance to strike it rich and escape the clutches of bean stew, bunghead.

Mrs. Karaghiozis: *(unseen)* Don't forget the thermos of bean stew for the journey. I've made a special batch for you – from Troisgros's grandmother's recipe.

Desert Island Wine

(Stavrakas enters.)

Stavrakas: Troisgros's grandmother's bean stew, is it? Did she use a finer bean than we grow? But here, Karaghiozis, this special-delivery letter came to the village for you today.

(Karaghiozis grabs the letter and reads it)

Karaghiozis: *(shouting to Mrs. Karaghiozis)* You had better make it a two-week supply. I'll be going to Arizona from Brussels. *(to Stavrakas and Hadjiavatis)* The biotechnologists can't squeeze wine from cactus and are calling me in as Advisor Plenipotentiary. But wait! I won't be here when the Vinexpo people from Bordeaux come. Do me a favor, boys, and help out when they bottle the cask of Local Stuff they've bought from me. They said it's the best wine that isn't wine that Euros can buy.

* * *

The chair, though superb in architecture, was upholstered in one of those flagrant chintzes, designed, apparently, by the art editor of a seed catalogue. I itched to have it reupholstered in some stout denim, but dared not thus affront the veiled unknown.

Alexander Woollcott,
"The Editor's Easy Chair," 1934

22

LAID BACK

Throughout recorded gastronomic history the most delicate of wine chatter has gushed from the cream of bibulous society caught in the act. Sophisticated verbiage can comfortingly compound excesses the less articulate members of society are content just to commit with grunts, gesticulations or reticence. It is not coincidental, for instance, that Plutarch and his companions discussed "Concerning the suitable time for coition" while at one of their protracted symposia. Reclining eases the burden and encourages a certain *savoir faire*. Pleasure is something we have always preferred to take lying down:

> Bdelycleon: …but lie down there, and learn to be convivial and companionable.
>
> Philocleon: Yes; but how to lie down?
>
> Bdelycleon: In an elegant graceful way.
>
> (Aristophanes, *The Wasps*)

Elegance certainly is most agreeably recognized horizontally, even if the observer happens to be vertical at the time. That's how I came face to face with it recently at the display window of a swank clothing store. Two sleekly attired, svelte female mannequins were gracing a highly polished mahogany dining table otherwise decorated only with a slim candelabra. One of the mannequins was placed lounging on its side, feline fashion, across the length of the table; the other, more filly than feline, was positioned with forearms on the table and knees on a chair seat, so that the small of the back curved sweetly inward and set the ever so spare buttocks in a fetching tilt.

Desert Island Wine

Who knows, perhaps the 'horizontal tasting' itself stems from such obsessions with elegance.

But we lack a comprehensive history of humankind by which to date key developments in the history of wine appreciation. Even so, the role of hedonism in the emergence of vinous elegance is suspect. Hedonism's root is in the Greek *idys*, or 'pleasurable,' which was used in the expression *idys oinos* as we would use 'fine wine': "the sweet strains of the muse, and *oinos idys* in Boeotian cups" (from the 5th century B.C. poet Bacchylides). The expression *idys oinos* developed from the figurative sense of *idys* as 'sweet.' The Romans went on to employ the Latin term *suave* in places where the Greeks used *idys*, as when Cato mentioned one wine as "mild and sweet [*suave*]."

In applying *idys* to flavor imagery, the ancients had to invest it with a connotation that could be grasped intuitively. But in this case the grasping had to be marked more by what could not be perceived than by what could be. In other words, it had to convey the impression that the human organism is in no way taxed by the object of its delight. Otherwise the wine might nip at the palatal heels, perchance spoiling pleasure: "...there will be as much [wine] as we desire, and it shall be very sweet [*idys*], too, with no teeth in it, already grown mellow, marvelously aged..." (Alexis, *The Dancing Girl*, 4th century B.C.).

The word elegance itself did make an appearance in classical literature related to wine, but only once, and even then with only the broadest of meanings. In the 1st century A.D., the Roman Pliny addressed a passage to the wines of the Spanish provinces and mentioned that certain areas were known for *elegantia* of product. He was using the term strictly as a general indicator of high quality, not as a stylistic description, for he was comparing those areas with "the first vintages" (*primis*) of Italy, and he also apposed them to other Spanish vineyard regions known for quantity (*copia*) of product.

Elegantia echoed the Greek verb *eklego*, which had been compounded from *exo* (out) and *lego* (to pick, select, choose). The Romans used the very same Greek building blocks, *exo* plus *lego*, to construct the verb *elego*, which they used just as *eklego* had been by the Greeks: "At the vintage the careful farmer not only gathers [*legitur*] but selects [*elegitur*] his grapes" (Varro, 1st century B.C.). Further, just as the Greeks had derived from *eklego* the term *eklektos* for reference to 'choice' quality, so also did the Romans derive *elegantia* from *elego*.

But it was only much later that the Romans gave *elegantia* a descriptive function for application to people, and still later that they applied it to objects of human use. As for wine in particular, both the Romans and Greeks persisted throughout antiquity in using as stylistic descriptions only terms that we recognize as participating in elegance, not the term elegance itself. When Athenaeus, in the 3rd century A.D., mentioned one wine as "very light and mild," he could well have been indicating a wine like the 1877 Bordeaux praised in 1932 by H. Warner Allen as "light, stylish wines, gifted with finesse and a delicate elegance."

Elegance as we know it in wine appreciation today essentially is a confection from the garment district of gastronomy. It is all about fabrics and textures: silks and satins and such. A critical development may actually have been the introduction of the word garb for costume. Garb derived from Italian *garbo*, which originally had more to do with Greta's kind of stuff than with clothing. Apparel and other accoutrements slipped in by a technicality: *garbo* bridged the notions of adroitness, a quality that cannot be ascribed to inanimate things, and gracefulness, which can be. Thus did medieval Italians begin using *garbo* as a wine description. For instance, the Venetians who controlled Crete applied it to Cretan light wine, *malvasia garba*, made in a dry and low-fat style from any of the various kinds of grapes more typically used to make the famous sweet Malvasia of the Middle Ages.

Material evidence tying these terminological strands back to antiquity is found in a letter of 1816 written by the early American enophile, Thomas Jefferson: "by our term *silky* we do not mean *sweet*, but sweetish in the smallest degree only" [italics in original]. Jefferson could not have come closer to the figurative sense of the ancient Greek wine term *idys* had he tried.

Still, elegance as a stylistic description did not come into fashion without some further tossing and turning on the cultural bed of wine appreciation. A decisive changing of the sheets occurred after France was attacked by phylloxera toward the end of the 19th century. Admirers of age-worthy French wines were nearly traumatized by the phylloxera episode, or more precisely, by the uprooting of vines and replanting on American rootstock which took place in its wake. It became an accepted tenet of wine lore faith that something irretrievable had been lost to the future because of it, or as H. Warner Allen put it, "I fear it means [the wines] have lost a little of their most exquisite polish." In practical terms it meant that the formerly expected additional finesse of an extra decade on an already ancient bottle would, as it were, die on the vine.

The regret was profound, and was manifested in an ornate manner of speaking about wines. Words became all the dearer to the connoisseurs as the bottles whose memory the words were meant to immortalize in wine lore became ever rarer. Allen wrote, "their keynote...is rather their pompous majesty than delicacy and charm, and they are still glorious in their old age" (in reference to the wines, not the connoisseurs). The tendency was compounded by the banquets of the day as nostalgia grew with each course – and the disappearance of yet another irreplaceable pre-phylloxera bottle.

Tongues were untied by phylloxera, and all manner of terms became fair game for application to wines. The particular weakness of this baroque connoisseurship was for words previously reserved for human traits or activities. Adaptation of that sort ideally accommodated minds conditioned by post-phylloxera regret to conceive of the surviving wines as veritable liquid personages, the better to sing their praises for all history:

> "Now shall we have the 1865? The 1865 Ch. Lafite, please, William...WONDERFUL!"
> "Yes, it is certainly wonderful, and what preservation!"
> "It beats me altogether. 1865 is it? Think! it has been over sixty years in bottle."
> "Incredible!"
> "But how soft and what a farewell."
> "Yes, and as you remarked, how marvelously preserved!"
> "Go on, go on! I delight to hear your comments; they make me feel a queer inexplicable pride."
> "Have you much of it?"
> "What! pride?"
> "No – of the 1865! The pride you can keep, but the 1865 I would like to share with you."
> (Charles Berry, *Viniana*, 1929)

Laid Back

While 'elegance' suited the needs of the times, it rose to its singular preeminence by becoming the exclusive stylistic term that could be identified with 'delicacy' and 'finesse.' This occurred through a defrocking of other descriptive terms of praise habitually applied to competing wefts and weights among vinous textures. Foremost among these terms was the onetime encomium *corsé*. André Jullien in 1816 had defined *corsé* wine most favorably: "wine which has body...a certain consistency, a pronounced taste, a vinous force, whose substance is [fleshy but firm], which fills the mouth." He went so far as to appraise the best red wines of Hermitage, which he classed with the best of Bordeaux and Burgundy, as "*corsé*, fine, and delicate."

But in the decades following phylloxera, *corsé's* similarity in sound to coarse caused it to be pressed into use as a vivid foil term to elegance among Anglophone enophiles. For instance, in his 1920 classic, *Notes on a Cellar-Book*, George Saintsbury related an anecdote about a wine merchant who advised him of an 1869 Richebourg: "Yes, it's great in its way; but it's a *coarse* wine" (emphasis in original).

Corsé naturally became associated with vinous gabardines, corduroys and flannels in the usage of a generation of connoisseurs who derived a warm glow from the pride they felt whenever they detected the esteem with which their sheerer wines, much like raiment from the gentler cloths, were beheld by anyone gauging their position in the social fabric. By the 1970s, *corsé* had become terminally tainted and was thrown in with terminological bedfellows that Jullien would have found very strange indeed: "*corsé* red, flabby white, sugared rosé."

'Elegance' has narrowed our conception of delicacy. Jullien's understanding of 'delicate' wine was more inclusive: "it is neither harsh, nor tart, and can have some spirituosity, some body, and even a certain *grain*, but those qualities must be well-combined, and with none dominating." Further, Jullien defined *grain* as "a kind of harshness [*aprêté*]...without having anything disagreeable." This notion of *grain* as a kinesthetic sensation had been around since at least the early Greeks, and had a shared origin with 'grain,' the planted food. The Greeks found that wine, even after it had become a particle-free beverage, might still vaguely recall the granular 'irritation' of the dilute grain drinks that were common in their diet; and indeed, their descriptive for coarse wine, *khondrós*, clearly was tied to their term for gruel, *khóndros*.

I find myself wondering about Homer's otherwise unspecified Divine Drink. Would it necessarily have been the unrelieved experience in unobtrusiveness – no, seamlessness – that we think would qualify it as Elegant?

When the ancient Greeks launched the term character, which literally signified a 'notching,' they comprehended that individuality of flavor can stem only from nudging the palate into some particular groove, lest the taste of a particular wine be confused with that of others that had sloshed about the mouth cavity to no certain effect. Sensations of tactile impact, even some irritation, were indispensable. Well, even amidst all of today's homage to the cushier wines, some enophiles mostly pay lip service to elegance and then tiptoe off to clandestine liaisons – rarely mentioned to their *confrères* of the cork – with some bottled paramour that does an attractive bump and grind in their chamber. Perhaps the deeper secret is that pleasure and pain sometimes do a mean tango together:

> Socrates: ...You are declaring that pleasure and pain are felt at the same time when you say that a man drinks when he is thirsty. Or does this not occur at the same time or place, whether in the soul or body, as you prefer? I fancy there is no difference. Is this so or is it not?

> Callicles: It is.

> Socrates: Yet you state that it is impossible for a man to feel pleasure while in pain.

> Callicles: Yes, and I say so again.

> Socrates: But you have admitted that it is possible to feel pleasure while in pain.

Laid Back

Callicles: It looks that way.

Socrates: Then to feel pleasure is not to fare well, nor is to feel
pain to fare badly. And the result of this is that what
is pleasant [*idys*] is different from what is good.

(Plato, *Gorgias*)

*   *   *

Dedication: To the newly liberated, formerly Marxist-Leninist wine makers east of Vienna.

23

FELLOW TRAVELER

Hey! Good to see you! I'm glad we could get together before you take off for Bolgoovia next week. A lot's been happening there wine-wise since communism ended, and I'd hate for you to come back complaining about the wine scene without knowing what you're talking about – although that never stops anyone else.

*

Fine, now let's get to the table and the tasting I promised you. We can deal with all your preconceptions later.

*

WINE #1

It's funny you anticipated that. As a matter of fact I thought about starting off with a Bolgoovian chardonnay. But what would that prove? And what challenge would there be in it for you? – either for your taste buds or for your psyche. Better you be exposed to the native grapes. Bolgoovia is a long way to go just to coddle your palate. You're not going over there and order *pâté* instead of eggplant caviar, are you? Someone as globetrotting in the kitchen as you are shouldn't be a stick-in-the-mud in the cellar.

*

No, of course I'm not "opposed" to the Bolgoovians growing chardonnay. For all I know it could be a good grape for some locales. And in a few places it might even give us a better picture of a facet of chardonnay that we are too little familiar with – which makes for a distinctive Bolgoovian chardonnay really worth having, not just a cheap one. Besides, chardonnay may be a nice change of pace for the Bolgoovians themselves. But I'd like *you* to feel the same way about native varietals like this.

*

Call me myopic, but it's always looked to me as though you can enter the European tradition of wine through its 'eastern door' just as well as its western. The fact that the West has never known much about Bolgoovian varietals and wines has historical explanations and doesn't mean there hasn't been an estimable past. I'd loan you several books on the subject, but they're all in Bolgoovian, which is one reason our wine writers can't tell us much, either.

*

WINE #2

Yes, it is produced by a cooperative. Just because the communists are out doesn't mean the old Bolgoovian aristocracy is suddenly going to make a comeback and a lot of titled names are going to start appearing on labels. Is that what they need to get your attention? Maybe that explains why Bolgoovian wines are always found collecting dust in some far lower corner in our wine shops.

*

That's true enough. There *are* small private individual producers cropping up here and there. But I'll tell you what: Anytime you can specify for me the telltale organoleptic features by which I can distinguish an estate wine from a comparable cooperative wine harvested from particular vineyard parcels I'll be all ears. I've got to warn you, though, that I'll hold you to a pretty rigorous standard on your explanations. Don't think you're going to get by with some mushy talk about 'polish' and 'breed' or what-have-you. I'll want to hear about 'what is felt where' in the mouth cavity; and I'll expect you to take into account any differences in the age of the vines, in *terroir*, and so on. Yep, I think I'll be a long time in hearing from you on that.

*

WINE #3

So, what if it *is* semi-dry? You never raise that 'issue' with Vouvray, to say

Desert Island Wine

nothing of Rheingau. Come to think of it, this is probably the sort of dinner wine the Germans wish they could always be sure of making without having to resort to sugar.

*

But wouldn't you say that the only relevant question is whether, as a semi-dry wine, it is balanced? I mean, look, let's take cucumber salad (since we'll be having some later). There must be several basic approaches to making it, and one is the sweet-sour angle. And nobody asserts that one approach is less worthy than the other, much less that one is more suited than the other to the nature of the cucumber. We just find the focus different as far as the equilibrium of savors is concerned. What's different here?

*

You are determined, aren't you? What do you mean, "this wine doesn't fit into your menus"? With all those exotic dishes you cook?!

*

I'll tell you a funny story about this wine. About 20 years ago it was being imported by an outfit in Texas and distributed in Washington, D.C., along with several other Bolgoovian wines. I was in touch with the Bolgoovian agricultural counselor at the time, and when the wines were on sale at a very good price I mentioned it to him during a phone conversation. The next day I went down to the store to buy some of this one for myself but couldn't find any. So, I went to the clerk and he tells me, "Somebody was here today – I think it was the Bolgoovian ambassador – and bought it all." And the wine writers in those days were always saying things like, "Those communist Bolgoovian wine makers are making semi-dry wines for the Russian market." The least they could have done was talk to a few Bolgoovians.

*

WINE #4

I can't sympathize with you at all on that score. This wine has body and firmness, and heaven knows, good red color (I can still show you the stains

140

on the wall where I accidentally cracked a bottle of this against it 20 years ago). The only "failing" you're speaking about is that it's not quite like any of the wines you're used to drinking.

*

What do you mean, "bizarre"? I don't see that its flavor is any more "bizarre" than that Provençal wine you opened last month – and you had nothing but praise for that one: "ultra-distinctive," you called it. What makes you think that if someone from the other side of the world tasted the two of them they'd agree with you as to which one is "bizarre" and which one "ultra-distinctive"?

*

That reminds me of the wine writer who tasted this wine while in Bolgoovia and commented something like, "This wine is interwoven into the fabric of the culture it comes from and will never enjoy a market outside Bolgoovia." Hmph! As if we in the West have somehow transcended the human condition and our wines don't reflect the prejudices of our cultures. Actually, the only circumstance that's different in the case of our wines is that the cultural and gastronomic contexts are implicit and do not need either explanation or comment. But pardon me, it was not my intention to get sidetracked on the subject of our gustatory imperialism towards Bolgoovia.

*

Don't get me wrong. I was never under any illusion that this is *grand vin*. But whenever I was really in the mood for it, nothing else would do – not Bordeaux, not Rioja, not Dão, not even Aglianico del Vulture – nothing. I guess for me it has been truly irreplaceable – and that has been my major reward in bothering with Bolgoovia. Let's see … what wine writer said that "endless variety" is what it's all about? Whoever it was, you can bet dollars to donuts he or she leaves that thought behind when it comes to Bolgoovia.

*

Anyway, you don't need to shy away from this varietal while you're in Bolgoovia. The cooperative in the meantime has privatized and brought in one of those airborne Aussie enological consultants. He's 'succeeded' in transforming this wine into a high-quality example of humdrum cross-cultural flavor – the writers are heaping compliments on it already.

*

Hah! I admit I must be a cretin of some sort where Bolgoovia is concerned. But what's your excuse with Provence?

*

WINE #5

Yes, a limited-production wine. You thought they weren't produced in communist times? It may have gone against their professed ideology, but not their proven lusts. Wines like this were made for the bigwig commissars and for international wine contests. The average person had no access to them. They weren't exported, either. If they weren't from familiar Western grapes, Western buyers wouldn't have been interested anyway. And our wine writers certainly were not going to risk their reputations and acknowledge 'communist Bolgoovian wines' of this quality – that would have gone against *their* ideology.

*

I'm surprised to hear you repeat that. Do you believe everything they write? Just because they're expert on France or California or Chile or wherever doesn't mean they know beans about Bolgoovia. Do you think they ever actually get to know Bolgoovian wines? I mean, do you imagine they cellar any? Do you think they drink any particular bottling more than once? Or that they even give them much more than a-sniff-and-a-gurgle trial? The last thing they need is yet another country to track. It's bad enough that New Mexico and Rhode Island came along. Even now it's a lot easier for them just to refer to Bolgoovia's "recent communist past" or drop in once in a blue moon and declare that "progress is slow." They want to 'fulfill their duty' to readers and be done with Bolgoovia, and then get back to Beaune or wherever it is they really want to be. I think of it as the fly-by-night approach to Bolgoovian wine.

Fellow Traveler

*

WINE #6

I'm glad you said 'superb' instead of 'super.' It may seem innocuous enough on the surface, but when you've listened to the connoisseurs or read the writers a while you come to realize that there's all the difference in the world between an utterance of superb and an exclamation of super: 'Superb.' goes with French berets and seriousness; 'Super!' goes with Bolgoovian kalpaks and insouciance. So called 'wine appreciation' is one of the last unchallenged bastions of ethno-racism, if you ask me.

*

I'm sorry it's not several years older, but I don't have a vintage backlog of it anymore. It wasn't on the U.S. market for over a decade. The present importer wanted to bring it in several years before the commies got the boot, but in the meantime the Bureau of Alcohol, Tobacco and Firearms decided it would no longer approve the label because it depicted an ancient Bolgoovian statuette with bare bosom. It was the Reagan-Bush years, you know. Anyway, the importer persuaded the new winery management to come up with a label that BATF couldn't object to. But I find the shape of this bottle rather voluptuous and suggestive.

*

I hope you can join me in drinking another bottle of this in four or five years. The 1979 when it was around 10-years-old was so good that at times I didn't know whether to laugh or cry that none of our wine writers had found it and brought it to light. And at $2.50 a bottle it should have been neon light. Flavor would pour out of that wine for as long as you could roll it around the mouth and not swallow. It had all the extravagance and none of the forbearance of coitus interruptus. It was more obscene than the label. When this wine is ready I'll send a bottle to Senator Crackpot and the Moral Majority to get their opinion.

*

Desert Island Wine

Maybe so, but why should I give any credence to what she has to say about it? Where Bolgoovian food is concerned, she's in the same boat as her wine-writing counterparts. I ran into her once at a Bolgoovian Embassy wine-and-food occasion, and I can tell you for a fact that she can't keep giouvetch and goulash straight.

*

Well, I wouldn't care except that some of our profound thinkers on wine are going to say there cannot be a real tradition of 'fine wine' in Bolgoovia since there is nothing but peasant cooking. They should know half as much about it as they want you to think they know.

*

Drink whichever wine you like with these. I think I'll go with the semi-dry. And by the way, while you're in Bolgoovia I don't think you'll mind the semi-dries at all with one of those zesty sauces from sour cream or yogurt.

*

Okay, so go for the yogurt and not the sour cream if you're really that concerned about your health. And you can even drink Bolgoovian red wine with it, especially if you focus more on the filling than the topping – maybe not *these* reds, but before you go I'll write down the names of some others I'd choose.

*

I'm glad you like them. You might not find them in restaurants – or at least I didn't in communist times. It's an unusual recipe for stuffed vine leaves that I got from an old-time Bolgoovian petite bourgeoise, Auntie Olga. I wish our gastronomes could eat at her table before opening their mouths about Bolgoovian food.

*

Fellow Traveler

WINE #7

You don't have a sweet tooth?! Who do you think you're kidding? I've seen you polish off desserts that make me ill just thinking about them. I've never known you to demure when the Sauternes comes out, either.

*

Try these dry-cured olives. They're vaguely 'sweet' and taste great with this wine – you'll see. And besides, it's the only dessert you're getting.

*

Of course the Russians were a great market for Bolgoovian dessert wines. But this one actually enjoyed a fine reputation and market in Western Europe in the late Middle Ages. We've long forgotten about that. Hmm, wasn't it some famous communist who said, "History is how you write it" or something like that? Our wine writers certainly used to subscribe to that where Bolgoovia was concerned.

*

You know something I've never understood? It's that the same Western wine writers who were so negative about 'the Russian palate' when writing about the Russian market for Bolgoovian wines, were brimming with puffed up pride when talking about the Russians of an earlier era who were great customers for Sauternes. Is that selective memory, or what?

*

This bottle's got a history. (You'll get a kick out of this.) It's left over from a small shipment of wines I sent by freighter from Bolgoovia some years back. I had to drive up to Staten Island to pick them up. The dock boss there started talking to me about wine and said he'd been reading about it in the newspapers for years. And he'd concluded, as he put it, "That's a lot of horse manure about this or that wine tasting better with some food." So there you have it from the dock boss at Holland Hook. And he ought to know, because he's handled more wine in a single day than you or I will see in a lifetime. (And if you believe he said "manure," I've got some fabulous pre-communist Bolgoovian wines to sell you.) Here, have another olive.

*　　*　　*

24

BLIND SPOT

Nothing could be more damning of me as a contemporary enophile than the difficulty I have applying the latest rallying chirp of wine folks, 'Drink less, but drink better.' Drinking less is not a problem as such, but I always end up drinking more trying to determine whether I am drinking better. I suffer from Quality Recognition Deficiency Syndrome.

Enophiles as well as other gastronomes with this condition perhaps are more basically flawed in being too modest in their demands where quality is concerned. I detected just such a tendency in myself several years ago when I became a regular customer for a strange brand of orange marmalade that suited my taste and also was priced beneath my means (because more discerning consumers knew better). The same thing has also happened with mustard and honey and olive oil and vinegar. In all these instances I reckoned quality according to my reading of what the thing essentially is and whether it has a personality of its own in that category. Beyond that I have been complacent in allowing unbridled subjectivity to take me for a ride. And when I do, I seem rather predictably to slide down to somewhere around the 75-85 percentile of objective quality – in other words nothing worth my preening over.

Where wine is concerned, I should be able to do better despite my disability because I have been reading about wine quality since 1971. At that time I was no more likely to seek advice about quality in wine than in marmalade, but I bought a wine book in order to have vicarious wine experiences while at sea with the Navy, and immediately in the introductory chapter I was hit with a section called 'The Quality of Wines.' This completely changed my frame of mind about wine. Beginning with my very next port visit I was no longer able to drink wine without wondering about what rung of quality I might be on, as if that were the most important thing about my relationship to a wine.

Later, even after I was ashore permanently, I continued occasionally to choose a book over a bottle. And if there is one thing I can say about this body of work, it is that wine literature has been preoccupied with quality differentiations for a long time. Pliny was already focused on them in the 1st century A.D., when he wrote about wine in his *Natural History*. But quality-challenged persons like me can at least bear Pliny because he made allowance for us. Or anyway he was given to providing the salt with which he wanted to be taken on quality. For instance, he related an anecdote about the Emperor Augustus's visit to a certain nobleman, when the Imperial wine taster had to select a wine from the host's cellar and wryly predicted that Augustus would be attracted to one wine in particular, even though it was not one of the best of those sampled. The Imperial taster could just as well have been talking about me.

Alas, Pliny is too remote both in time and attitude to be a role model for today's wine commentators. Quality has been taken much too seriously for my handicap ever since André Jullien's *Topographie de Tous Les Vignobles Connus* hit the stands in 1816. Jullien was imbued with the scientific spirit of his age, and he constructed a mesh of categories and quality levels by which to classify and rank the entire then known world of wine. Exhaustive rankings of one degree or another have been with us ever since. In fact, it is what passes for intellectual rigor in the genre. Not to be uncharitable – I am only caught up in the spirit of the evaluation exercise – at least it does allow wine literature to rise occasionally to the third or fourth rank of intellectual pursuits, which still leaves it well behind philosophy and theoretical physics, though at times its codifications and appraisals raise it close to law and accounting.

A person in my condition is bound to be awed by wine rankings of Jullien's breadth. If I consider the number of wine regions – to say nothing of individual wines – I cannot imagine how I should ever manage to classify all of them qualitatively during my entire lifetime. Of course I am presuming that one cannot assign a region or a wine to a quality class without being thoroughly familiar with it; and as far as I know this can only be done credibly by actually drinking and considering each on its own (not in the context of comparison tastings), and doing so on repeated occasions. But perhaps this view is just symptomatic of someone with Quality Recognition Deficiency Syndrome. Fully functioning tasters, especially those whose opinions count in Winedom, may not see it that way. Jullien, for one, was so sensitive to quality criteria that he was able to classify many non-French wines confidently on the basis of secondhand and even third-hand tasting notes of a cursory kind left by travelers to the regions concerned. Rivaling him in gumption, today's writers manage to inspect and make certified declarations of quality about ten unfamiliar regions and 100 previously untried wines in a single morning.

Blind Spot

But I am impressed that wine literature has been consistent in clinging to just a handful of cardinal levels of quality. The first book I read broke quality down into four tiers, and you may imagine my surprise when I found that Pliny had done the same nearly two millennia earlier. Even Jullien, who put a finer edge on the analysis of vinous characteristics, came up with only six levels. However, there was a significant difference between Jullien and Pliny, in that Jullien gave indicative names to his quality levels: Fine; Semi-Fine; three levels of Ordinary; and Common. This innovation gave rise to our subliminal drive to identify our taste preferences with the higher ranking word ("Could anything *Ordinary* really appeal to *me*?"). Meanwhile, persons with Quality Recognition Deficiency Syndrome, while feeling this need no less than anyone else, blow their sensory fuses when trying to distinguish, say, Fine from Semi-Fine, or Ordinary from Common, or any one rank of Ordinary from the other two.

But even if Jullien's actual rankings still exert an anonymous influence on how regions are gauged, his indicative names have not stood the test of time. He probably doomed himself to irrelevance on that score by failing to tag any level Great. Jullien did indicate that wines occasionally might surpass his top level of Fine (we might suppose this was his implicit category of Great), but this was a determination he expected buyers and sellers to make. He was skeptical about anyone being able to specify criteria by which to recognize such wines fairly and consistently. Events bore him out, because the notion of Great Wine did not get its hammerlock on us until the Bordeaux Classification of 1855, which was a commercial device of the first rank.

However, we are also distant from Jullien on the other end of his quality spectrum, the Ordinary levels, which he regarded better than the quality we would be inclined to impute to them based on that name. Jullien followed a much older tradition of the term Ordinary as an indicator of something done right, in the Latin sense of 'by the rule,' whereas we are persuaded by the pecuniary connotation of 'ordinary' as 'cheap' (although, paradoxically, this demotion of Ordinary wine seems only to increase our fond attachment on certain occasions to the term *vin ordinaire*).

Our wine writers are unconsciously replacing Jullien's old terms with ones to which we can relate more readily. Today's enophiles are more savvy about wine than their predecessors in Jullien's time, and want quality levels that catch all the nuggets of wisdom on quality that the writers scatter among their jottings. But Jullien's successors do not subject themselves to his degree of discipline when it comes to setting out genuine organoleptic criteria of quality, if they try to specify any criteria at all. This is extremely disorienting for those of us with the Syndrome, and in order to help myself in the face of this obstacle, I have been keeping and collating notes from the popular wine press regarding the current evolution in the terminology for ranking wines. As a result, I have compiled a 'cheat sheet' by which to get around my failing and be able to guestimate quality without appearing an utter fool in wine society. From lowest to highest, I have been able to discern seven contemporary de facto levels of quality, and I recognize them as follows:

VIN ORDINAIRE:

Name Connotation: Wines produced for just anybody.

Tell-tale Characteristics: Rough around the edges.

Circumstantial Giveaways: Tastes acceptable only when nothing else is available.

Deception Threats: Any of life's ordinary circumstances (otherwise known as 'sensory interferences') can treacherously result in overestimation of these wines.

Word Association: Plonk (Note: Due to technological advances, authentic plonk is rarely produced commercially nowadays. Vin Ordinaire will have to do.)

FOOD WINE:

Name Connotation: Wines whose winy-ness benefits from food accompaniment.

Tell-tale Characteristics: Slightly perceptible flavor that peters out in mid-taste.

Circumstantial Giveaways: Cumulatively takes on the flavor character of any food it accompanies.

Blind Spot

Deception Threats: Can seem expensive when paired with foods that are better than it deserves.

Word Association: Nondescript

ETHNIC WINE:

Name Connotation: Produced chiefly east of Vienna, but potentially in any winery where no major European language is spoken.

Tell-tale Characteristics: May have aroma and flavor, but not of a kind we recognize.

Circumstantial Giveaways: Never complements Classic or Nouvelle cuisine, and may facilitate pronunciation of appellation or grape names that lack vowels.

Deception Threats: Wines of this rank can taste seductively ambrosial when offered by persons attired in apt folk costume.

Word Association: Eccentric

SIPPING WINE

Name Connotation: Wines a little too expensive to be gulped.

Tell-tale Characteristics: Nice structure, and crisp, crisp, crisp.

Circumstantial Giveaways: Just enough personality to be identifiable in a blind tasting, but not enough to think about at any other time.

Deception Threats: Overly charming when served on patios or sundecks; doubly so at sea-side.

Word Association: Amusing

Desert Island Wine

HAND-CRAFTED WINE:

Name Connotation: Recalls pre-industrial era wines of quality as we like to remember them.

Tell-tale Characteristics: Subtle edges turn smooth in finish.

Circumstantial Giveaways: Wine novices mistake its character for faults.

Deception Threats: Goes too well with bean casseroles for its own good name.

Word Association: Genuine

WORLD-CLASS WINE:

Name Connotation: Wine that anyone anywhere would recognize for high quality.

Tell-tale Characteristics: Remarkable stylishness.

Circumstantial Giveaways: Stands up to visual and aromatic inspection against a background of white tablecloths and pastel kitchen aromas.

Deception Threats: Can seem of lesser quality if sipped during the soup course.

Word Association: Serious

GREAT WINE:

Name Connotation: Wine that stretches the imagination.

Tell-tale Characteristics: Indefinable symmetry and a finish that goes on and on and on.

Circumstantial Giveaways: Makes you drink slowly and thoughtfully.

Blind Spot

Deception Threats: Because of its delicately poised balance, Great Wine
may be mistaken for Ordinaire if food is served.

Word Association: Gorgeous

But these guideposts are no more than that. They will not carry
me very far in these times when wine is increasingly viewed as just another
object to be measured. Greater precision is wanted. This can be seen in a
variety of techniques that the professional wine troopers are trotting out to
enhance our ability to rank. For instance, enologists recommend timing
persistence of mouth aroma (aka 'length') with a stopwatch; and one wine
writer suggests stretching a tape measure from the nostrils to the surface of
the wine in the glass so as to measure intensity of bouquet.

But while these toolbox solutions may answer the needs of normal
enophiles, I am at a loss in recognizing the split-second at which a sensation
becomes a perception, and again when it ceases to be one. This must be why
some enologists would prefer to remove my limited sensory contribution
from the exercise altogether by devising neat equations that convert raw
data about wine to elegant qualitative values, as in the 'suppleness index':

$$\text{alcoholic strength} - (\text{total acidity} + \text{tannin})$$

The beauty of such equations is that they yield objective figures,
perhaps even several decimal places' worth of objectivity. I am nevertheless
frustrated in applying the results to the actual rating process because it is
unclear the extent to which any particular index value is a universal indicator
of quality, as opposed to a mere regional indicator of quality. The dispensers
of the equations surely are not suggesting that anyone – let alone those
afflicted with the Syndrome – attempt a direct comparison in all respects
between two different kinds of wine.

I have my fingers crossed that a more sanguine remedy may be on
the horizon. I am encouraged to think so because gastronomy currently is
on the road towards intersecting with medicine. The French Paradox and
related findings promise that wine will be included, and this could result in
a comeback of the Hippocratic standard of quality. Hippocrates, in an early
version of 'drink less, but drink better,' thought that the right amount of the

appropriate wine for one's present condition is the only 'best' wine. His view of the worth of vinous qualities was, as it were, an internal one: "Food and drink which, though slightly inferior, is more palatable, is preferable to that which is superior but less palatable" (*Nature of Man*).

The prospect of a physiological inspection and consideration of wines in addition to – or in place of – a sensory one does present great challenges, and it may not go down well with our hale pundits. But for someone in my feeble sensory condition, it may be the last hope of having any say in the quality assessment game.

*   *   *

The anonymous personal wine advisor known only as Mr. Corky has won a dedicated audience among a worried – and some say worrisome – segment of the Dionysian public over the past several years. He has been called the Zorro of Winedom by his fans, and the Prince of Wine-Darkness by his detractors. The following samples of his no-nonsense, cutting-edge guidance are taken from www.pullingyourcork.com, with permission of the webmaster.

25

MAIL CALL

Dear Mr. Corky,

I have finally met an attractive woman who knows chardonnay from charolais. My problem is that over my years of bachelorhood and gourmandizing I have put on a bit of extra weight and tip more toward charolais than chardonnay on the scales. I feel self-conscious about it because my lady friend has managed to stay trim and fit despite an avid interest in wine and food. I think I need to lose about 40 pounds to have a shot at long-term happiness with her. But dining out and dining in are two of our mutually favorite activities, and I am no glutton for workouts. Do you have any hints for enophiles who want to lose pounds without shelving their wine glasses?

'Need to Shed'
Hackensack, New Jersey

Dear Need to Shed,

Rest assured that it can be done. You might start by storing your wines at a troublesome distance from your table and with some obstacles to getting at them, so that you'll think twice about getting up to retrieve a second bottle. Ideally that would be a cellar with a trap-door over which you can place a largish rug (so you're not reminded by sight of the door) and a heavy piece of furniture (so you'll not want to bother moving it). Then, when selecting a bottle for your meal, just go along with your friend's instincts, as the last thing you need is to have two competing bottles on the table. As for training yourself mentally, you will ever have to keep in mind that wine encourages appetite, no matter its presumed quality. I recommend two measures, though you might have to put your enophile status on hold for the duration of your weight-loss program. First, adopt the akratisma of the ancient Greeks and take wine-soaked bread for breakfast – as much as you can stand. (You didn't say whether you are retired and face midday temptations. The akratisma would be the perfect solution for that.) What might be harder to swallow is a regimen of wine-food combinations you don't like, at least when dining alone (you don't want to put your friend's latent affections to too strenuous a test too quickly). If you don't know many 'bad' combos, consult the weekly and monthly wine critics; they maintain long lists of them.

*

Dear Mr. Corky,

My husband and I are torn between two wine tasting events on the same Friday evening next month. One is a tasting of Burgundies sponsored by a Burgundian wine firm and their importer, at $40 per person, and the other is a tasting of new-age kosher wines from seven countries being held by a local synagogue, at $80 per person. My husband is Jewish and liberal, and thinks we ought to give the kosher wines a try. I'm agnostic and skeptical, especially since the kosher tasting costs twice as much. My husband says I'm being narrow, parochial and non-thinking traditionalist in my outlook on this. But actually, I think he might be hopelessly optimistic. What do you think?

'On the Fence'
Flint, Michigan

Mail Call

Dear On the Fence,

What I mostly think is that either the congregation is still paying off its mortgage, or that the Burgundies are made at least in part with concentrated must. It's hard for Mr. Corky to say more since he is unfamiliar with the Flint wine scene (but apparently the overall economic picture has improved since the last appraisal by Michael Moore). Because of the uncertainty involved here, my inclination is to go along with your husband on this and take the cosmopolitan internationalist track. For one thing, then he won't be able to escalate the labeling war that's going on between you two and call you a retro-eno-chauvinist or worse. I would be far more definite in this advice if I knew that the kosher wine tasting is part of an oneg shabbat spread. That way you could think of the occasion as an opportunity to find out which varietals you like best with corned beef on rye. All religious beliefs aside, finding that out is nothing to sneeze at in this life, and in the long run it might be worth a lot more to you, as an enophile in the U.S, than the Burgundy tasting. Besides, I have to be devastatingly frank and warn you that at the Burgundian tasting you would be lucky to get third-rate gougères to nosh on.

*

Dear Mr. Corky,

This is a terrible confession for an enophile, but I've always felt overwhelmed by the many kinds of wine from so many different countries. I've never been able to get over the fear of being embarrassed around my enophile friends if I didn't know all of those wines or couldn't keep them straight or couldn't even pronounce their names. But at least I used to be able to exclude various countries from my field of interest by striking a self-righteous pose and refusing to buy or taste wines on political grounds, like when I wrote off Chilean wines during the Allende years, or when I boycotted my club's tasting of Soviet Georgian wines by saying they were made with gulag labor. But the political face of wine has changed so much in recent years that my arguments don't hold water anymore. Let's face it, I can no longer indignantly refuse to attend tastings of East European or South African wines. I worry because I'm retired now and can't keep pace financially. I'm really sweating to remain wine solvent these days.

Desert Island Wine

'Self-Limited Horizons'
Phoenix, Arizona

Dear Self-Limited Horizons,

The first thing is to get past your apparent guilt, and to understand that you were not alone all those years. It was quite commonplace in your generation of enophiles to write off wines for ideological reasons. It was a viewpoint willy-nilly encouraged by the high-profile connoisseurs, and it did trickle down to the rank-and-file, even though most of them remained quiet about it. Looking at the present and future, it's clear that you will have to reassess your foreign policy, so to speak, because really all that's left of the old world order in wine today is Algeria, and in the future maybe China if Wal-Mart opens that cellar door. So if you need to continue being an exclusionist enophile, whether from fear of inadequacy or fear of impoverishment, the trick is going to be in finding some bugaboos other than political ideology. For instance, you could refuse wines from countries or regions that have offended some newly realized environmental or animal rights sensibility (how do you feel about run-off from bacon-farms or the force-feeding of geese?). Or, you could continue ignoring eastern Europe, but now for other reasons, such as the oppression of their Roma populaces (you're not partial to Liszt's 'gypsy' tunes while sipping Tokaji, are you?); etc. Just remember this verity: Publicly defensible excuses are always at hand for the thinking enophile to remain self-limiting geographically.

P.S. At your age, I'd beware of being too wine solvent and over-sweating in Phoenix.

*

Dear Mr. Corky,

I'm a 51-year-old wine aficionado facing a crisis that I don't know how to handle. I've always been very discriminating when it comes to combining wines and foods, but in the past year I seem to be enjoying all combinations about equally. The thing is, I can still assess wines – I'm almost always within three points of my newsletter's scores – it's just the combinations that throw me for a loop. I take a bite of the food, and it's like my critical faculties turn off and some inner hedonist beast takes hold of me. I could be in danger of losing my aficionado status and have had to stop hosting dinners for wine friends. Sometimes I think I might be in the early stages of dementia.

'Flagging Senses'
Sag Harbor, New York

Dear Flagging Senses,

Whoa! Let's filter out the dementia business. And while you're at it, you might want to use a finer mesh and stop pegging your aficionado-hood to newsletter wine ratings. The latter aside, I'd say your prognosis actually is pretty rosy. First, you've got at least another quarter-century before you need to fret about your powers of discernment going significantly downhill. Second, the chances are that good sense is kicking in for you whether you want it to or not, and in a most timely way, too. Take my word for it, most aficionados don't start showing sense until way too late in life (and the elite never do). Your misdiagnosed 'predicament' shows us why the ancient Greeks and Romans did not spend much of their short time on earth worrying about wine and food combinations: By the time they were of age to drink wine freely, they could already see their demise just a decade or two down the pike. So, forget dementia and just remember to savor fully while you still can, whether for better or worse.

*

Dear Mr. Corky,

Something terrifying happened to me a couple of weeks ago at a wine tasting. It was all the more surprising because I was conducting the tasting and had chosen each wine to make a point. But as I looked into wine #4, all of my knowledge began shedding from me like an old coat of hair. Before I knew it, there was just the wine and me. I was unable to separate my being

Desert Island Wine

from my senses. I had not come face to face like that with a beverage since malted milks at the corner soda fountain as a child, and as comfortable as I was with the feeling at the fountain back then, that's how petrified I felt now at the tasting. I managed to go through the motions of the tasting mechanically, but I stayed on that metaphysical plane until midway through wine #6, when the spell broke as suddenly as it had started. Just two days before, I had finishing reading *Zorba the Greek*. I'm feeling really sorry that I read it. Are my days as a connoisseur at an end?

'Transported'
Port Gamble, Washington

Dear Transported,

Ah! yes, Zorba. I'm surprised you experienced such terrific results after just one reading (it took me four to have an experience like yours). The book should be required preliminary reading for any course of wine study. There is no dearth of respected authorities (you know who they are) to whom you might turn for instruction on wine, and they stand ready to hand you all sorts of crutches on which to hobble through the world of wine with full security. But I would sooner take a page from Zorba any day. He had cut the ropes from which we habitually dangle like puppets, and thus had no catechisms to recite, no verbal prisms to refract his sensory experiences into neat categories where things would lay forever fixed. Zorba had arrived at a place that most of us moderns do not dare reach: the union of body, mind and spirit. It is the startling and intimidating intersection where the confining and suffocating walls of certainty collapse – and it is also the abyss where wine is best tasted. Do not be dejected. Nay, someday you might be dejected that the incident you describe was the only time you ever truly came to grips with wine.

*

Mail Call

Dear Mr. Corky,

I'm pretty new to wine. I started converting from beer about a year ago. My cousin has been drinking wine a long time and is trying to guide me. He's even been taking me along to his monthly wine club meetings. I appreciate it, but the thing is, he and his friends always seem dismissive about my preferences, or at least amused by them. According to them my picks are always "too off" (or maybe they mean "two off" – they use scorecards, so I'm not sure). And they use language I don't quite understand to tell me where I'm going wrong. I don't know what to say back and just keep my mouth shut. My cousin says I'll eventually get the hang of it. But I'm discouraged and beginning to think I don't have the right instincts for wine. Maybe I just belong in beer and bratwurst.

'Mum's My Word'
Milwaukee, Wisconsin

Dear Mum's My Word,

Anybody who can tolerate a nagging pack of wine weenies as well as you have done these past months has won half the battle. I do not think your "instincts" are any worse than anyone else's, certainly not your cousin and his friends. There is a question in my mind, though, that you may be a little too sensitive about wine talk. If you're going to be a social, public enophile, you've got to get used to the fact that enophiles are forever saying all sorts of stuff totally unselfconsciously and non-personally – and not infrequently maddening. You've also got to understand that words ultimately drive the industry, from the largest wine factory to the smallest garragiste. You could try pressing your cousin and the others to explain what they mean more fully, which nine times out of ten will leave them sputtering or obviously winging it (you'll be amused either way if you get over your anxieties and insecurities). But if after another year or so you find that you can't take the heat of wine wind, you can always retreat and become a closet enophile who explores wine privately and silently. There are thousands of them roaming the wine store aisles and scouting out the shelves even as I write. Actually, they're the ones who keep the industry afloat through good vintage and bad, even if they always keep their distance from 'best' wines and have nothing against wurst.

161

Desert Island Wine

*

Dear Mr. Corky,

My wine merchant keeps trying to sell me on a costly brand of wine glasses. Where it really gets expensive is that he tells me I need all the shapes of glasses in the line if I'm going to get the most out of my considerable investment (with his guidance) in my wine cellar. His explanation is that I'm paying for the *terroir* in the bottles but will not get all the *terroir* that's coming to me unless I have the very best and most appropriate glasses. He also says that if the stemmed versions of the glasses are absolutely beyond my finances, I should at least get the versions without stems. I'm reluctant about the stemless kind because holding them feels too much like having a water glass in my hand, no matter the *terroir*. Is there any way out of this dilemma without offending my wine merchant?

'Glass House'
Swampscott, Massachusetts

Dear Glass House,

Let's work from back to front on this problem, meaning: let's start with your stem fixation. It's nothing new, but at its worst (and you seem about there) the notion that not having stemmed glasses will void your experience of wine can be debilitating for your morale over the long haul. That includes your determination to bring sensory perception rigor to bear, and thus could even interfere with your appreciation of terroir, which after all is your merchant's talking point on glassware. Besides, just consider the pickle you'll be in if you ever have to drink wine from a tumbler with the actual inhabitants of a terroir that truly offers all that the term trades on. So, the first thing I want to suggest is that you start drinking wine from water glasses for a while. Trust me, if you can't <u>honestly</u> – and that's the key word here – pick up on terroir in a plain glass, there's none coming to you, no matter the wine's price, repute, or score – or what your merchant has to say about it. Second, you ought to can that merchant lest he take your heirs to the bottle cleaners before they ever see a cent from you. He seems to have you by the stem.

162

Mail Call

*

Dear Mr. Corky,

My New Year's has been starting off on the wrong foot wine-wise ever since my father-in-law ('Rex') died. My mother-in-law ('Dora') makes prime rib for New Year's Day dinner, as she always did, but never pours anything but white wine with it. Not only that, she took offense when I brought a red, and wouldn't let me have the corkscrew. It's a real shame because her prime rib is great, and her whites would be impressive with other food. My wife suggested she cook something else, but Dora says her family has been doing prime rib since forever. I've tried explaining that red wine cuts through fat and protein, but Dora just glares at me. My wife thinks it's because Rex was a boardroom bigwig who always opened classy Bordeaux, even though Dora never cared for red. But why should the rest of us have to suffer on New Year's just because she still holds a grudge against Rex?

Bound and Gagged
White Plains, New York

Dear Bound and Gagged,

It's sad to hear of wine causing unhappiness. Your fallback mental stance should ever be: any good wine is better than none. As for Dora's wine choice, don't assume anything, because wines and personal memories are a complex business (her whites might represent something that only she and Rex knew about). Instead, give more thought to the 'cutting' principle. It has an air of stuffy men's clubs about it, and with rare meat and red wine we also get into blood and atavistic hunting rituals. Without doubting the validity of male-bonding over beef and Bordeaux, it is amusing that writers go on and on about the nuances of a red wine, yet take a one-dimensional view of its pairing with red meat, namely, 'cutting' fat and protein. It's almost simplemindedly hedonistic (which can't be faulted if you are not claiming the higher palatal ground). Since you like Dora's whites otherwise, go for a well-done slice of prime rib and focus on the aromatics of the combination. But since considerable temperature contrast between wine and food can cloud aromatic perceptions, praise Dora on her wine choice while suggesting she serve it less chilled. If she glares, either palm your wine or fan your beef – and enjoy!

Desert Island Wine

*

Dear Mr. Corky,

I was in Montenegro on a private trip several months ago, and when I visited wineries they treated me like a dignitary once they found out I work for BATF [Bureau of Alcohol, Tobacco and Firearms]. In fact, the government export agency was told about me and insisted on shipping me a couple cases of the country's best wines, which hardly ever leave Montenegro. I thought I'd share them with the little wine club I belong to, and so I held a blind tasting of several for the group, alongside some famous Western wines of comparable color and body. The two highest scoring wines of the evening were Montenegrin, even though the eight tasters had about 140 years of collective wine experience. But when the wines were unveiled, the group was aghast and there was a lot of recanting. The oldest taster said he'd "rather have the name wines, the world-class stuff any day." I'm thinking about leaving this tasting group.

'Baffled and Ticked'
Washington, D.C.

Dear Baffled and Ticked,

Look, wine lovers pride themselves on being generous with their bottles, but to be generous with praise for the underdog, even when deserved, comes hard to some, especially those who cut their teeth on Bordeaux, Rheingau or Napa wines decades ago. So, yes, you goofed in sharing your windfall bottles with this group of wine folk instead of a Balkan folk dance club. But you might think twice about parting company with them because it sounds as though their sessions are a blast, an essentially harmless opportunity to observe enophile silliness. But at the same time, you might scout around for a club of similar size but with half the collective years of experience, so as possibly to have weeded out well-honed pomposity to some extent before you open something rare and 'exotic.' After all, you seem to be in a position to be the recipient of a lot of vinous largesse overseas if you keep traveling to wine countries and playing your card right – and I do mean your BATF calling card in particular. (Mr. Corky must confess to jealousy of Grand Cru magnitude.)

*   *   *

164

26

An Egyptian merchant dealing in papyri and other manuscripts has made available the following translation of what he claims is a lost chapter of Aristotle's *Problems*, which was rescued from the destruction of the Library of Alexandria by an ardent ancient enophile and passed down through the generations among his descendants. The merchant has never been charged with fraud, and the present chapter bears the marks of authentic Aristotelian puzzling. [*A summation in contemporary terms follows each puzzle.*]

PROBLEMS IN CONNECTION WITH WINE

Why do men become drunk from drinking wine, whereas the gods do not become drunk from nectar? Is it because the respective natures of the gods and of nectar are each whole, whereas those of men and of wine are not? Things that are whole may fuse as one if they are of a compatible nature; but they do not mix by exchanging parts since things that are whole are neither divisible nor soluble. But the respective natures of man and of wine are each incomplete and they assimilate to one another by mixing and solution, which proceed through confusion. Wine's nature is hot and has, in a manner of speaking, an ardor of spirit because it is vinous; whereas man's spirit is his least substantial component, so that vinousness, as its presence in him grows, burdens the process of mixing and thus adds to the confusion he may experience from imbibing.

[If a man has his head together, he will take wine piecemeal.]

Why are courtesans who habitually drink the dark and dry wines more provocative to men than those who do not? Even sober men say it is because the courtesans who drink these wines have a more earthy and sultry smell. Is this because the astringent component of the wine overcomes the moist element that characterizes a woman, and thereby forestalls the effluence through her pores of waste from the sweet essences intrinsic to her? For this would explain how the earthy element in her perspiration achieves a more perceptible exit than in the case of women who do not drink the dark and dry wines. Conversely, the odor of women who habitually indulge their taste for the moist in sweet wine and olive oil is compared by men to hydromel and is said to lack pique.

[Bouquet is best appreciated filtered through a courtesan.]

Desert Island Wine

Why does the flavor of a wine persist longer in the mouth when it is drunk with certain foods? Is it because like flavor unites with like, so that the two flavors grow in strength? Even after swallowing, both give the impression that some essential part of them is still identifiable, though not separable, one from the other, in this perception. This is demonstrated by the practices of makers of sausages, pickles and confections in choosing herbs and spices that complement their meats and fruits. But nobody makes this claim for wine when it is drunk with plain fish, as wine has in it no flavor that partakes of fishiness, unless indeed it is salt itself. But salt has no distinguishable fragrance to bond with wine, and vinous flavor does encompass aroma.

[Wine-food combinations should be taken with a grain of salt.]

Why does a wine need to be presented at a particular coolness, whether more or less of it, in order to be at its most pleasing? Is it because wines are hot to a varying extent? Wines vary in heat because their moist and dry parts are arrayed variously. These parts in a particular wine must mix with the air in a suitable proportion until they assume the arrangement that nature intended; that is the arrangement which maximizes the wine's vinous properties in a conformation that differentiates it from another wine, for therein rests its particular quality. But this depends on the condition of the air with respect to coldness, for air is the agent for mixing, and its coolness, or lack thereof, regulates the extent of mixing. Those whose profession is to mix wine and water hinge their success in the first place on the condition of the air in that respect, since in addition to the nature of the wine they must also have in view the nature of the water.

[Not all ice cubes chill all wines to equal effect under all conditions.]

Why are the intoxicating effects of resinated wine delayed compared to other wines? Is it because man's access to the intoxicating part of wine is inhibited by resin? Wines mixed with salt water hasten intoxication because they are drying and this is not natural to the body. Sweet wines that are otherwise similar to certain austere wines, particularly in their heat, are slower to intoxicate because they are also moister, which is more natural to the body; and resin participates in sweetness. Those who eat wheaten bread

Problems in Connection with Wine

when they drink wine also get drunk less quickly than those who eat barley biscuit, since wheat is more glutinous and therefore more sweet and moist than barley.

[Fresh-water baths with resinous courtesans are the best venue for wine drinking.]

Why is the soft palate struck by some vinous fumes but not by others? Is it because some fumes in the wine are propelled by a power independent of vinousness? The soft palate must be touched by something that has substance, but the properly vinous fumes have presence without force and merely float in the atmosphere of the mouth. Or is vinousness accompanied by some other, unbridled element that will not float in the mouth, but instead propels itself upward as though to separate itself from that to which it does not belong, and thus encounters the soft palate? This element must reside in the lees when they are still fresh, for the sensation occurs in young wines, which are unsettled, but not in older ones. Indeed some wine growers hasten to separate the new wine from its lees, in which they believe its youth lies.

[Some wines cannot be swirled enough.]

Why is one wine heavier than another? Is it because the heavier contains more earth? Sellers of water demonstrate this to be the case with various waters when they weigh them, filter them hard and weigh them again. But this cannot be the sole explanation in the case of wine since some wines are heavier than others and yet the lighter wines may have an earthier smell. But the smells of some earthy substances can neutralize one another, and this may happen in a wine irrespectively of its weight. Similarly, truffles are separated by smell as well as by size, and hunters are at pains to train their animals to find those which have an earthier smell no matter the size.

[Weigh a wine carefully – you may want mineral water instead.]

Why does its color create expectations as to a wine's general nature yet provides no sure demonstration of its specific flavor? Does this occur because of a certain deficiency in the human sensory apparatus, such that the eyes are, as it were, blind to the perceptions of the senses of taste and smell? Our ability to interpret nuances of earth in wine by the wine's color is hampered because earth has no liquid form by which we may train our observation to associate shades of color with the nuances of flavor in liquids. But the specific taste of a wine cannot be attributed to earth alone; were it otherwise, the shading of solid fruit itself would give no clue as to the flavor qualities that people do in fact detect first through their eyes. The explanation must be that because wine scintillates and recalls the sun, the eye is most fascinated by this scintillation because its powers emanate from the sun; and therefore it resists the visual distraction of mere color gradations.

[The earthiness of courtesans cannot be gauged in daylight.]

Why are dark wines preferred to white wines in winter? Is the dark color, being associated with that of fire, related to our visual desire for fire during the cold part of the year? This seems to be so, since white wines are observed to be as much in possession of the element of fire as are dark wines of congruent consistency – and both may support a flame in the same degree. Meat roasted at the hearth in winter is also more appreciated than fried viands. For although both offer the diner a similar inner heat, the memory of the hearth stokes the mind's eye with a greater impression of warmth even as the physical eye surveys the hue of the roasted meat.

[A wine will only taste as good as it looks to you.]

Why does fermentation bring earthiness forward in wine? Little or no earthiness is perceptible in the juice before it becomes wine. Is this because the earthy savors are held in the skins of the grapes? The fruity sweetness of grapes lies in the pulp and this is consumed by the bubbles that are engendered by the ferment. But the skins are also attacked in this process. But the earthy components are only detached from the skin, and so dissolve in the fermenting juice; whereas the fruity essences of the pulp in part escape in the air and in part are muted in flavor by the transformation that occurs. And the result of this process is that the first [earthiness] grows in perceptibility while the latter [fruitiness] recedes.

[The de-stemming of grapes for wine making may be overrated, depending.]

Problems in Connection with Wine

Why does 'vinous' not suffice as a description of wine? Is it because the term is something of a misnomer? A variety of qualities are subsumed under 'vinous' and yet it cannot be a sum since its parts do not always add to the same result. It must be, rather, a collection, however random, of related elements. Some waters are called vinous, and some of these actually may produce a condition resembling intoxication. But such waters lack a majority of the features found among the liquids properly called wine, and their intoxicating quality indeed may owe to properties that do not participate at all in vinousness. Yet wine can never be other than vinous.

[Even the headiest mineral waters will carry you but so far.]

Why is the bouquet of a wine when it is mature perceived at a greater distance from the bowl than when the same wine is either young or old? It must be because the various fragrances composing the bouquet, having lost their tendency to wander from one another, combine in a kind of unity whose resulting strength penetrates the mist with greater cohesiveness and is presented to the nostrils intact. For in the young wine these fragrances have not been able to establish their commonality and they begin dispersing almost at once from the surface of the poured wine; while in the old wine this unity, which is now fragile, is steadily torn asunder by the air as the bouquet rises through it, since the air easily attaches to itself one by one the weakest aromatic links, as though it were plucking the petals from the bouquet.

[Either youthful or aging courtesans will tend towards flightiness.]

Why is a wine found most pleasing at the locale where it was grown? Is it because the atmosphere where the wine originated assists its fragrance? Does the local air conceal the less pleasing aromas of the local wine? The heavier part of the air at that site may appropriate and carry downward and away from the nostrils the heavier scent in the local wine. But this would deprive the wine of its most characteristic aromas and leave it an expression only of its fruit and not of its locale. Is it, on the contrary, that a kind of synergy is created when the wine mixes with the air of its native place? The heavier part of the air defines the character of the local atmosphere and is drawn upward together with the lighter part because it is intrinsic to that place and so does not sink there on account of its heaviness as it might elsewhere. But while doing so it also assimilates the heaviest part of the wine's aroma, because the latter derives its nature in part from the same local atmosphere and therefore is compatible; and then it brings all this into the nostrils in the lightest, most pleasing form.

[Inhale deeply if you happen to be tasting a wine outside its region of origin.]

Why do fishermen, returning at dawn with their catch, happily drink sweet wine with their meal upon the beach, yet not want such wine in the evening? Is it because the equilibrium of water and salt in them changes according to the time of day and their work? Apparently so, for in the morning they are 'brackish' after their night at sea and also are eating fish, whose flesh is the kind most influenced by salt. Salt thus seizes the fishermen both from within and from without and makes them peculiarly in want of that which is wet but not salty. Sweet wine satisfies this need to a greater degree than other wine since it is moister and more quickly restores in the fishermen their natural equilibrium.

[Do not judge wine except when you are in balance.]

Why is the first wine drunk at a symposium perceived to be more in possession of wine's fire than those that follow? Is it because of the olives served as hors d'oeuvres? The olives, because of their oil, reduce the sensation of fat in the wine, so that the wine's heat is more apparent. But the same sensation of pronounced vinous fire occurs when trying the first wine at a merchant's shop where no olives are proffered. Confections of honey also taste most potent when first tried, as indeed do spiced olives, and so forth. The characteristic part of the taste of a food or drink, because it must be set in relief relative to its other parts, makes the strongest impression on the taster until his body's equilibrium is inured to this defining sensation.

[Order your wine sampling prudently, leaving fiery courtesans for last.]

Why do mountain folk prefer their hard and dry wines and shun soft wine? Is it because the altitude at which they live dries up their watery part, so that their palate detects more of the moisture and less of the dryness in their wines than when those wines are tasted by people living lower down?

Problems in Connection with Wine

In a parallel way, even laborers at the low altitudes find tart dark wines best suited to their state after returning in a sweat from the fields, since their mucous then is thick and they feel less of the astringency and more of the wetness of these wines. Thus, too, men of substance who are exposed neither to manual labor nor to the elements bear neither the tart wines nor the hard and dry ones without complaint and lectures about vinous harmony.

[The sociology of wine appreciation never changes.]

*   *   *

27

WINE'S EYE VIEW

"Oh-oh, they're choosing me. It's stage time. Hey, I'm way too young for this. I'm still in my violet bloom. You couldn't want *me*. Take this guy over here – yeah, go ahead and take *him*. He's been sleeping like a brick since way before you stuck me down in this hole of a cellar. For Pete's sake – and for mine – look at the vintage date on him. Just open him up and have a gander at his rim – its browner than his label. From the looks of him, he could be a corpse, in my humble opinion.

"Whoa! Whoa! Easy up the stairs, now. No skipping. I'm unfiltered and there's a lot of stuff in me that you couldn't see if you tried. I'm prone to seasickness and nose bleeds, and at the rate you're going you'll find it out soon enough when you drink me.

"A sideboard?! Only an imbecile or an enophile would have a sideboard in this day and age. How long am I supposed to stand here, anyway? And who *are* these other green-glass dudes? I don't recognize their labels. This better not be what it's looking like.

"Oh, sweet Bacchus. Yes, it is. A tasting. And I'm batting third. You mean, I've gotta endure two bottles' worth of sports and sex metaphors before my act? Ain't that just the pits?! I'll be worn away to my ash before I get a chance to strut some stuff. And that must be the designated slugger to my left. Batting clean-up, eh, Sammy? Why don't you just take your sloped shoulders and go flex somewhere else. No, on second thought, I can tell from the quality of the conversation at this table that you're just about their speed, intellectually speaking. They couldn't sniff their way out of a brown paper bag. Must be a nest of wine journalist wannabes. SOMEBODY! GET ME OUTTA HERE – QUICK!

"Hey, perv! What's that you're sticking in my ear? I'm being violated! The word spread through the cellar about your kind. What was that noise?! Who let in the light? My anthocyanins are all a-tingle. Where are my shades? Pass me the smelling salts while you're at it – I'm not ready to be oxygenated. Is this some sort of pagan sacrifice of virgins, or what? Wine needs empowerment, is what I say. This is America, isn't it? And you don't see any flubs in the English on this label, do you?

"Just listen to it fly. You should be ashamed of yourselves, carrying on like that. It's only wine, you know. Like, just how good do you think it's going to get? If you want to look into the face of God, or whatever, take yourself to Mount Athos and eat beans in olive oil with stale whole-wheat bread for three months. And you over there, knock off the Meg Ryan routine. If you keep it up with the faked orgasms you'll make me lose my lunch – and any sensations I might hold in store for you.

"What kind of *year* did *I* have?! You've got to be kidding. 'What kind of *day* did *you* have? is more like it. I'll bet your boss chewed you a new grommet. Your sweat is still showing through your shirt, by the way, and that scent you doused yourself with before coming over here isn't helping either of us perform worth a damn. Believe me, a wine isn't going to give any better than it gets. And just so's we're clear about it, I sure as hell ain't giving it up for the likes of a toiletries junkie like you.

"Listen, fella. That's my *terroir* you're jumping on and you're obviously way off home base. In fact, you're out of your league altogether. Just stick to what you know and we can both keep our dignity. Yeah. If you wanted plum jam and flue-cured tobacco you should have kept me in the cellar another five years, fool. And you've got a lot of nerve questioning my cleanliness. You should see the half of what I'm seeing. It's like a gustatory Armageddon in here. You call this a mouth? Shall I do a show-and-tell: tuna fish wedgies to starboard, two-day-old cumin seed fragments in the port crevices, barbecue chip shards scattered fore and aft. You want I should continue? You certainly are one 'complex' sewer viewed from my perspective. But the real rub is that you want to go rubbing it off and blaming it on me.

" 'Elegant' is it? You want *elegant*? Look, Bub, I didn't promise you no rose garden, so don't go pinning your self-stroking expectations on me. What you should expect is that I could help you with overcoming your hang-ups and rigidities. But I can't do it if you're not going to meet me halfway – truth is, practically all the potential between you and me to be what we're not lies with you. I'm afraid the ball's in your court and I can't fill in for you, so stop asking me to.

Desert Island Wine

"You'd *better* lap me up. And make the most of me, too, while you're at it. You could at least pretend that you're capable of enjoying me. No wonder you don't get any dates and end up spending Friday nights in mortuaries like this. But I didn't have any business being here in the first place, and am I ever feeling used. All I've done is sacrifice my tannins to make Bozo here look good. After the deposit I've laid on your palate, Sammy's gonna feel like Grand Vin to you – and a lot of thanks I'll get for it. And to think, I've got legs enough to stand on my own if I'd been given half a chance. I could have wowed you guys. I could have gotten a four-star score. I could have been a *contender*!"

* * *

28

ONE ON ONE

A wine lover's nightmare became reality for me one day when I walked into the room where my wines were stored. I was looking for a wine for dinner and discovered that there were none. This was not literally true, for in fact I had nearly six cases of wine. But what amounts to the same thing for a wine lover, none of the wines was 'ready.' All still needed years of aging, and if I opened them I would instantly lower myself from eno-phile to eno-philistine. I thought of old Charlie from the wine club where I formerly was a member, the time he and I had been chatting about our wine cellars and I mentioned that over a period of several years I had whittled mine down from 700 bottles to about 200 currently. Upon hearing this last figure, Charlie, with all his years of experience weighing in, lowered his chin, fixed me with a distressed look and said in a doomsday tone of voice, "That's not enough." I was dumbstruck at the time, but now, standing before my few remaining cartons, I suddenly knew what he was getting at.

My first impulse was to head out to a wine shop and buy three or four cases of wines that were 'drinking.' Few of them would be duplicates, either, because several years earlier I had been persuaded by a do-it-yourself aficionado like myself that buying more than three bottles of any specific wine can only set back one's aficionado-hood. Wines after all are many, while life is short. Yet I found myself flashing back through my recent years with wine and had second thoughts about this policy and the course of action I should take in response to my unforeseen supply crisis. For the fact was – and it was hard to admit it – I was less appreciative of wine than I had once been, and this discomfiting loss seemed a direct result of my mania to try places and grapes and producers and vintages. I was sure that only a radical adjustment might help me out.

The non-enophile wine drinker (which is a distinction that needs to be made) might not relate to my predicament. Even though I was not in the same class as the major league wine writer who bristled when he thought I might be doubting his familiarity with a backwater appellation far off his usual wine routes ("Are you suggesting that I have not tasted X?"), I was nevertheless at home with a variety of wines from around the globe. To be without any selection of wine at all was, therefore, not just an inconvenience, it also posed me with an identity crisis.

Desert Island Wine

It is vinous philandering that sets the cosmopolitan enophile apart. We may in all other departments tend towards monogamy, but through years of consorting with a bevy of wines we become habitually inconstant about 'whom' to invite up from our cellar harem from day to day. Familiar with the charms of many, we have a palpable inkling most evenings of whose, in particular, we want in our chamber. This is also the vice that marks our character compared to our fellows with other frailties. And I, for one, had held a profound respect for vices ever since my college days, when the local candy store owner, a pipe enthusiast, told me from behind his aromatic cloud of smoke that everybody needs one. Not only was I determined to cultivate a vice, I also wanted to feel that I deserve credit for it, and as an enophile that meant variety galore.

But over the years my determination had landed me in surfeit, even if only modestly so. I could not yet emulate the eminent elderly connoisseur seated at my table at a wine dinner in London once, who flatly announced to the table that he had not enjoyed any of the six wines served. My major symptom was, instead, that in opening bottles I was often driven by compulsions of various kind that went beyond just a healthy curiosity. To be sure, this is not a disgrace among enophiles, and it may even work to lend one an aura of formidable knowledgeableness. But I felt nonetheless that my compulsiveness was a threat to an identity even deeper than my being an enophile, for I was no longer approaching wine in the matter-of-fact way I consider most natural to me.

Abstinence, I already knew from several Lenten experiences, would not resolve my condition. Even the greatest playboys and playgirls among enophiles could endure a period of celibacy. No, it would take a much more rigorous discipline, a real enophilian hell, to cure my bibulous enervation. This, I decided, could only be a regime of drinking the same wine day after day. Other enophiles might talk about their 'desert island wine' – the wine they would choose to have if all they could have was one – but I would actually try it for a spell.

But which wine to choose?

My first thoughts went back a dozen years to Mrs. Schukopf, the single mother of my daughter's first-grade friend. Mrs. Schukopf also had two other children, and she seemed perpetually harried from juggling parenting and a job as a night-duty nurse. But she always had a partially empty jug of the same brand of wine standing on the floor of her kitchen – definitely the mark of a non-enophile wine drinker. I thought of following her example and going to a supermarket to decide on a jug, or else to a wine shop to pick something in .750 liter bottles from the lower bins. The problem with this was that I could no longer pretend I had no conceptions about wine and go back, in effect, to Square One. Suppose I honestly could not take a liking to the wine. It would be perverse to persevere with it. Obviously even Mrs. Schukopf had been sticking with something that pleased her well enough in her price range.

But at the same time I did not want to choose a wine that impressed me overly much. I had absorbed my share of quality consciousness from wine literature and was afraid I might undermine my goal if I were able to bask in quality that I knew self-styled connoisseurs would concur in (for this may be the most widespread form of wine snobbery, practiced nearly as satisfyingly alone at home as out among other enophiles). Instead I needed a wine about which I could have no respect of forethought. Fortunately for the integrity of my venture I had recently begun sending a third of my monthly income to a college and simply could not afford objective quality gratification as a steady diet.

A wine that met my tough requirements and was available locally came to mind quickly enough. I thought of it because the last time I could recall responding to a wine in an unfettered way was two vacations previously when I had drunk this same wine in the region where it was grown, as a cosmopolitan enophile occasionally will do. For that very reason I hesitated momentarily about selecting it since my happy firsthand memories of the place it came from might sometimes get the better of my good sense about the wine. But I decided that even if that should happen on occasion it was no more than the same sort of psychic putty used routinely by other enophiles to fill in the chinks in quality when drinking more prestigious bottles that are not really up to form. The overriding fact was that I was *never* going to be comforted by any delusion that my chosen wine might gain the respect of other enophiles. That much was hammered home for me when I went to the store to buy my first case and the wine consultant remarked with a bemused sniff, "I never sold a case of that before."

Desert Island Wine

Actually my wine had several shortcomings going for it to keep my emotional response to it realistic. To begin with it was made from a grapes-of-wrath variety. Those are the grape varieties whose existence is acknowledged somewhat begrudgingly because of something unpalatable about their geographic origin or presumed stylistic suitability that does not allow them to tickle the fancy of anyone in the know. (It is why one wine super-mart boasting 472 cabernet sauvignons and 550 chardonnays was carrying not one example of my varietal.) This was related to the wine being of the 'ethnic' stripe, which cosmopolitan enophiles are accustomed to think of as the vinous equivalent of panpipes and bagpipes, as opposed to the string quartets gathering dust and crust in our cellars. How fitting, too, that my wine could claim only 'Country Wine' status, which usefully added to its bumpkin image in my own mind.

Compounding its dubious varietal and geographic origin, the wine was produced by a cooperative. Nothing in the history of wine ever struck so much fear into cosmopolitan enophiles as has the notion of putting grapes under the feet of confederated peasants. The Bolshevik era that gave rise to this mindset was already several years in the past, but my estate-fixated brothers and sisters in cups preferred perpetuating the hysteria because it makes it that much easier to dismiss many increasingly well-made wines that might broaden flavor horizons and encourage subversive free thinking about varietals and regions.

My wine was not only ideologically incorrect, it was also white. I once heard a lecturing wine writer tell her audience that she never feels contented when dining if no red wine is served – and that was *before* promulgation of the French Paradox telling us that we should drink red wine if we care at all about our health. But from my perspective the only remarkable aspect of my choosing a white was that it was already going on winter, the season universally averred as the one preordained for red wine. Further, although (obviously because of a personal quirk) I like certain white wines in winter, chilled and all, my chosen wine was not like any of those. But I decided that this inappropriateness of season might serve to restore some of the adversity that was lost by my having chosen a wine that I like. I might even be tempted from time to time to abandon my resolve prematurely, which was the most adversity I could hope for in a trial of this gravity.

One On One

Choosing a wine and starting to drink it on a daily basis proved the easy part of my test. It was much harder to get into a frame of mind for a ritual cleansing. I had always been a label shopper of the kind who is attracted to a scene or a design or a color scheme and buys the bottle to admire and muse about its label while also under the influence of its contents. Being that way, I was not immediately able to enter wine shops and survey the stock rationally. I continued to buy other wines rather impulsively as if I were going to drink them soon. Finally there came the day when I saw a wine that ordinarily I would have jumped for, and that I did think of buying on this occasion, but which, I realized later in my car, I completely forgot about by the time I got to the checkout counter with my father's beer that I had come for. This was two and a half months after I stopped drinking other wines, such was the lag between my attitude and my mentality.

Getting past the letter and into the spirit of my commitment was important to me. I was conscious of emulating the mentality of Grandpa Gócs, a hobbyist wine maker from Hungary who understood more about wine, as such, than I was ever likely to learn. He represented for me the inhabitants of Old World wine regions who are exposed to little variation in the kind of wine they drink. I remembered walking into a wine tavern in a small Hungarian town one Sunday afternoon when local men were seated around a table drinking the local wine and singing old songs. Paradoxically, it is wine drinkers like them, parochial 'enophiles' with a relatively narrow range of flavor reference, who created the distinctive styles of wine available to cosmopolitan folk like myself, and I wanted to understand something of their experience of wine.

I would like to have been able to replicate the conditions of an Old World wine region with its circumscribed gastronomic possibilities and unspoken codes. On that much I was in sync with the cosmopolitan's recent clamoring for sips that express the flavor of ever smaller units of production: *cru* or single-vineyard wine; single-malt scotch; single-grove orange juice. The full fantasy is to live on and feed off a self-contained piece of land, a micro-environment unto itself, so as to restrict oneself as much as possible to the gustatory limits of one's very own *terroir*. But I did not have the financial resources necessary to this exquisite daydream. During my single-wine regime I had to make do with an array of foods that would bewilder a provincial from an old wine region. In fact I called on my wine to serve with a far wider variety of dishes than was ever dreamt of by the peasants who for centuries had stuck by the grape I was drinking.

Desert Island Wine

The furthest I could go in confining my flavor universe was in adhering – more so than less – to The Mediterranean Diet. Enophiles had signed aboard as soon as they noticed the similarity between *cru* and cruet (*l'huile d'année est arrivé*) and concluded that the olive is as fit as the vine for serving up *terroir*. As gastronomic fortune had it, although I had started out from a Habsburg frame of flavor reference, I had been developing a taste for olive oil ever since third grade or so. That was when my mother started making a Sicilian dish of baked sausages, vegetables and herbs, all richly lubricated with olive oil, which she learned from her friend, Filomena. I could never leave the table without taking a crusty piece of Italian bread and mopping up the excess of aromatically infused oil in the bottom of the baking dish. I later graduated to a summer job in a Greek restaurant that bucked the pre-Mediterranean Diet sensibilities of Americans by daring to cook with olive oil, and I went on to become a shameless seeker of unapologetically olive-oil-laced dishes in Greece itself. By the time of my desert island wine trial these tendencies, both societal and personal, had led my diet largely into an ersatz Mediterranean groove – or about as narrow as it would ever be without my actually relocating to the far side of the Pillars of Hercules.

My wine was a Mediterranean white and I expected it to influence my diet – namely to push it ever further south. Enophiles, reading occasional anecdotal evidence in wine literature, are taught to expect taste preferences in food to accommodate themselves to habitually imbibed wines. This is all the more so if the wine has something special going for it in flavor. My wine actually did – and more so than its humble origins entitled it to. Its peculiarities even evoked for me just the right landscape for Mediterranean foods. But except for geographical mirages, I was never entirely convinced that my wine was more compatible, strictly speaking, with Mediterranean than with other foods I continued to eat. Just to give one example, although my wine did play to good effect against plain wheaten bread (toasted or not) moistened with olive oil (extra-virgin or not), it was equally good with butter spread on rye, provided the butter was salted and the rye caraway-seeded. At that rate, the adaptation of my eating habits to my wine was going to proceed at a glacial pace and the results might not play out in my lifetime.

Contrary to the expectation I had from reading wine literature, the more I warmed to my wine the more difficulty I had coming to conclusions about the relative goodness of particular combinations. Nor did I have any really solid guidance from the literature as to the criteria by which to rate one combination better than another. Sometimes a combination seemed truer to the individual partners yet not as attractive as either had been with other partners; sometimes a combination seemed better in mouth aroma than in mouthfeel; sometimes it was better after swallowing than in the front of the mouth; sometimes flavor contrast seemed more advantageous to the partners than flavor congruence; or the reverse situations. On top of that, my impressions varied according to the size of the mouthfuls I took, the pace at which I alternated the wine and the food, and the length of time that I was ingesting it all. Then there were the times when I found myself in a predicament like the one Zorba described (about lovemaking, not ingesting), of being "driven crazy" by a beauty spot and unable to fault it as a wart no matter how great the distortion in flavor. Those instances, though, were no more of a predicament than other enophiles find themselves in when it comes to chocolate or Roquefort or prosciutto with certain wines.

But I did detect that my needs in the way of wine-food pairings began simplifying. This must have been happening because of my increasing fascination with basic foods and flavors. Bread, for one thing, became much more important to my satisfaction as I continued with my one wine than it had been when I was drinking many. Indeed sometimes the nature of the bread made a significant difference in my view of the wine at mealtime. I would no longer agree, as I once did, with the cosmopolitan reviewer of an ethnic-wine book, who took the native author to task for dwelling to no purpose on several native breads since it obviously has nothing to do with wine appreciation. It might have something to do with it for provincials.

Food did more than its share in landing me on the final plateau in the ascent out of my enophilian pit. This was apparent at about the six-month mark, at Easter, when I baked a lamb and drank my usual wine because that was positively the wine I wanted to drink. I did think my white had a rare compatibility with the lamb, in aroma as much as in feel (which cannot even be said of many reds when you look closely); but the fact was that I had become so sensitive to the wine's features, that I was able to discern it, as what I knew it for, in virtually any guise that food might cast it in, no matter what else I might think about the combination. I would bet that the mono-cultural denizens of old wine regions do the same. Perhaps also like I was doing, parochial enophiles might compensate for lack of variety by milking the taste of their foods for new flavor perceptions of their wine. Certainly there is a lot of riveting complexity in it.

Desert Island Wine

It was also after this point that I completely lost my worst fear about renouncing other wines: that my powers of gustatory observation, such as they are, might decline as a result. I was conditioned by world-class wine lore to think that I could only sustain this capacity by constantly tasting and comparing a lot of divergent wines. But I discovered that any number of daily occurrences served to keep my gustative faculty alive since the environment offers many olfactory overlaps with wine and food, and can trigger the same motivation in us. And quite amazingly I was finding that a lack of variety could actually call forth a greater effort to exercise my inclination for perception. Sister Wendy had recently been on television preaching the joys of 'imbibing' one painting at a time; and even though I had never looked to enology for art I found plenty of substance to experience and reflect on by staying put in the gallery of my one wine.

At last I was breathing easy – all too easy for a cosmopolitan enophile. Some days I drank none of my wine at all because I knew when I actually wanted wine and when I did not. I also began to drink other wines again from time to time just as a parochial enophile may occasionally be treated to another wine and think no less of his habitual one. I was perfectly confident that a day or two or ten away from my wine could only increase my preference for it. An enophile friend with twice my years in the sport once observed that Great Wines do not usually make their distinction plain beyond a first glass, but here I was, quite the happily devoted monogamist finding the solidly distinctive qualities of mine in a second glass day after day, week after week. I was not yet confusing my wine with Great Wine, but I did start sympathizing with Pliny (*Natural History*):

> Who can doubt, however, that some kinds of wine are more agreeable than others…? And consequently each man will appoint himself judge of the question which wine heads the list.

*   *   *

Note to Readers: All kidding aside.

29

DISCOVERY:
CABERNET'S ANCIENT GREEK ANCESTOR

Along the Gulf of Corinth, on the heights above the Peloponnesian port town of Aighion, Angelos Rouvalis is cultivating vineyards for several varietal wines. He grows the widespread native roditis variety, but like many other Greek producers he has looked to cabernet sauvignon and chardonnay to win more attention for his efforts. At the same time, he is committed to reviving cultivation of two local heirloom varieties that had almost died out, the white lagorthi and red volitsa. Ironically, Rouvalis's unsung efforts with the volitsa would immediately rivet international interest for Greek wine growing were it known that a clone of this variety is an ancient ancestor of cabernet sauvignon.

Solid linguistic, historical and ampelographic evidence indicates cabernet's descent from volitsa. Only DNA confirmation is lacking. Of course, in light of the fact that cabernet sauvignon has been proven by DNA research to have resulted from a cross of cabernet franc and sauvignon blanc, the volitsa would be a closer ancestor of cabernet franc, and only a distant forebear of cabernet sauvignon.

Bordeaux is a long distance from the Peloponnesus, but classical literature provides information about how volitsa might have arrived there. In the 1st century A.D., Pliny (*Natural History*) mentioned a grape variety called balisca that he associated with Dyrrachium (now Durrës), a onetime Greek colony along the northern coast of Albania on the Adriatic Sea. Pliny's contemporary, Columella (*De Re Rustica*), mentioned the variety under the name basilic (basilica), and stated that it had only recently arrived "from far distant countries." Columella seems to have been referring to arrival specifically in the Latium region around Rome. Since Pliny said that the balisca was grown in "the Spanish provinces" under the name coccolobis (the Latin word for basilica the herb), it would seem that it had migrated from Dyrrachium to Iberia even earlier than it arrived on the Italian peninsula, or at least its western side. Thus, it might also have crossed the Pyrenees and reached southern Gaul before the 1st century A.D.

There has been occasional speculation about cabernet sauvignon having roots in ancient Greece. According to one theory, the balisca/basilica might have been the grape that became known as biturica in southwestern France because of the Celtic Bituriges who were settled around what would become the Bordeaux region and were engaged in wine growing there. By this scenario, the biturica would then have become, so to speak, the proto-cabernet, which would explain why the name vidure is an old synonym for cabernet. Although both Pliny and Columella mentioned the biturica separately from the balisca, the Bituriges might have misidentified and misnamed a cultivar of balisca. After all, Pliny clearly indicated that there were variants of balisca; and Columella tells us that even during antiquity "neighbouring peoples disagree in the names of vines, and their designations vary."

But whether or not there was such a link between balisca and biturica, various evidence points to the identity of balisca and volitsa, and to consanguinity between volitsa and cabernet.

Two aspects are key to realizing the ties of heredity. The most obvious is the confusion of *b* and *v* sounds caused by the Roman insistence on rendering the Greek *β* as *b* rather than *v*. The ease of confusing *b*alisca for *v*alisca during its early history in Western Europe can be understood from the later confusion of *v*iturica (aka vidure) for *b*iturica in France.

The second aspect that always needs to be kept in mind in reviewing the evidence is the geography of ancient Greece. For while Pliny presumably knew what he was talking about when he indicated Dyrrachium as the origin of balisca, he did not know that the variety had been traveling for centuries before that and had originated not along the Adriatic Sea, but along the Gulf of Corinth, in the same province of Achaïa where Angelos Rouvalis has resurrected volitsa today.

Cabernet's Ancient Greek Ancestor

The most dramatic suggestion of the consanguinity of cabernet sauvignon and volitsa comes from comparing cabernet's bunch and leaf as depicted in Jancis Robinson's *Vines, Grapes and Wines*, to the photographs of volitsa's bunch and leaf that appeared in *Elliniki Ampelografia* (Greek Ampelography, Vol. III, 1949; pages 84-89) by Vasilios Krimbas (incidentally, *V*asilios is *B*asil to us). It is like looking at the very same variety, right down to the leaf indentations. (See the drawings at the end of this article.)

But the pictures only underscore the descriptive notes on volitsa and cabernet sauvignon. The respective data given by Krimbas and Robinson demonstrate that both varieties have a leaf as wide as it is long; and a bunch two-thirds longer than it is wide. Krimbas describes volitsa's berries as small, with little flesh around the pips, and "skin slightly tough, red-violet, with bloom." Also, he gives the formal name of the variety as volitsa mavri, or black volitsa. This echoes Robinson's description of cabernet sauvignon: "the tiny dusty blue-black berries…have one of the highest proportions of pip to pulp." Although Krimbas describes the volitsa bunch as "compact," whereas Robinson refers to the berry arrangement in cabernet as "loose," no difference can be discerned between them at all in that respect in the pictures.

The volitsa, under the name vlosh, is still cultivated in Albania, and Albanian ampelographic information mostly chimes with Krimbas's description. In their book *Vitikultura* (Tirana, 1973; pages 567-568), Petra Sotiri, Todi Gjermani and Taso Nini mention a "compact" bunch, a "blow" covering on the grapes, and "tough" grape-skins. The photos of vlosh also look like Krimbas's volitsa, but the particular cultivar described obviously was not identical to Krimbas's since its skin color is described as only "bright red" and its wine is "pale" literally to a fault (the Albanian authors recommend deepening the color by admixture with other varieties, including, ironically enough, cabernet sauvignon).

However, the Albanian ampelographers indicate awareness of color variants of vlosh. Further, an earlier article by the Hungarian ethnologist Bertalan Andrásfalvy about traditional Albanian wine growing stated that both a "black" and a "red" vlosh were still being grown in southern coastal Albania around 1960 ["Formen des Albanischen Weinbaues," *Acta Ethnographica*, Vol. 1, No. 3-4, 1962, pages 293-373]. Andrásfalvy's information thus corroborates Krimbas's mention of 'black volitsa' and testifies to its presence in Albania. (Cabernet enthusiasts may rejoice that the right balisca was dispatched from Dyrrachium so many centuries ago.)

But it is Pliny who provides us some information by which to tie the modern-day volitsa to the ancient balisca. Already in the lst century A.D., Pliny was aware of two balisca variants, and his notes on them tally with the information about volitsa/vlosh. He did not specify skin color, but both of his balisca variants must have been dark-skinned since he commented that their wine can have a "rough [*austera*] taste," which suggests plenty of tannin. Especially significant is that he differentiated his two balisca variants by noting that one had "round" and the other "oblong" berries, which echoes Krimbas, who said that volitsa berries vary from "spherical" to "oval." Also, Pliny described the balisca as late-ripening and hardy, which the Albanian ampelographers also say of vlosh (and which also matches Robinson's notes on cabernet sauvignon). The one divergence is that Krimbas's volitsa buds and ripens earlier than those; but in comparison with Albanian vlosh, this could be the result of divergent cultivars.

As to balisca's geographic origin, the ethnologist Andrásfalvy believed that vlosh was originally a Greek variety, not Albanian. Obviously, the name *b*alisca is closer to *b*olitsa than to *b*losh. Furthermore, the Albanian language, coming from further east in the Balkans, did not reach its present territory (thus also at Dyrrachium/Durrës) until after the classical era. Even the Albanian ampelographer Sotiri acknowledged that vlosh was the Greek variety known anciently as basilika ["Vitikultura në Shqipëri" (Viticulture in Albania), *Buletini I Shkencave Bujqësore* (Agricultural Science Bulletin), Vol. 11, No. 2, 1972, pages 59-75.] Columella in fact had referred to the variety as basilica, not balisca. The name came from the Greek vasilikos, which means kingly or royal; thus, the grape name balisca was a corruption of basilika, not vice-versa.

But where in Greece did volitsa originate? The geographic distribution of the variety pretty clearly points to the northern Peloponnesus. It is notably curious that the variety is grown in Albania mainly in the southern coastal area between Vlorë and Sarandë (south of Durrës), but then altogether skips northwestern Greece (the province of Epirus) and does not appear again until much further south, in Achaïa, in the northwestern Peloponnesus. Further, Andrásfalvy cited an official Italian report of 1915 about Albania which mentioned that volitsa/vlosh was also grown just east

Cabernet's Ancient Greek Ancestor

of Achaïa in the province of Corinth [Gaetano Baudin, *Relazione della Commissione per la Studio dell'Albania*, Parte II. Le Coltivazioni, page 67]. It happens that Vlorë (or Vlonë) was the ancient Greek colony of Avlona (Aulon), while Dyrrachium, whence balisca was shipped to Western Europe, was founded by none other than Corinth.

But the ancient record suggests that volitsa's homeland might have been Corinth's neighboring province to the west, "the fruitful land of Achaïa" (Nonnos, *Dionysiaca*, 5th century, A.D.). Wine was the pride of the Achaïan city of Cynaethae from very early times, as illustrated by a remark of Pausanias (*Description of Greece*) on the inhabitants' hoary devotion to Dionysus:

> The most notable things [among the Cynaethaeans] include a
> sanctuary of Dionysus, to whom they hold a feast in winter,
> at which men smeared with grease take up from a herd of
> cattle a bull, whichever one the god suggests to them, and carry
> it to the sanctuary. This is the manner of their sacrifice.

Cynaethae just happens to be the predecessor of Kalavryta, the contemporary Greek seat of volitsa cultivation, just up the mountainside from where Angelos Rouvalis is perched.

Just how balisca lost its name in Western Europe is not clear. At Vinexpo '95, Greek wine grower Dimitris Hatzimichalis gave his view that the cabernet name is a corruption of carbonet and carbouet, which presumably were Gallic variants of the vine known to Pliny in Latin as carbonica ('charcoal'); and that the carbonica name had been derived from the Greek kapnios ('smoked') vine as a result of Greek colonization in southern Italy and the consequent production there of vinum fumosom ('smoked wine'), a name translated directly from the Greek wine known as kapnios oinos. Although Hatzimichalis therefore assumed that the carbonica vine must have been the balisca, the identity of the latter with volitsa indicates that the cabernet name could only have become associated with balisca through an inadvertent mix-up in the vineyards; or else a crossing of balisca with carbonica took place and only the latter's name survived.

Desert Island Wine

It certainly suits our image of cabernet's ancestry that basilika means royal. Moreover, Columella said that well-made "Basilic" wine can "attain the rank of nobility." Pliny similarly related that the Dyrrachians "speak highly" [*celebrant*] of balisca, and he commented that its wine can have either an austere taste that "turns sweet with age," or vice-versa, which sounds much like what has been written about Bordeaux reds since at least André Jullien in 1816 (*Le Topographie de Tous Les Vignobles Connus*).

Enophiles inevitably will want to compare volitsa wine to cabernet sauvignon. It does not seem quite fair to hold volitsa to the specifics of cabernet aroma and flavor since the two began diverging literally millennia ago. For that matter, without reliance on Krimbas's black volitsa cultivar, most volitsa wine, like that of Angelos Rouvalis, is going to be less dark than either cabernet sauvignon or cabernet franc. But maybe the final litmus test would have to focus on physiological effects since Pliny remarked that balisca wine is "very good for disorders of the bladder." Do we know anything about that for either of the cabs?

———————

Note: This article was completed in May 2006. In June 2007, Mr. Rouvalis reported that he has suspended commercial efforts with volitsa because of unsatisfactory results at his growing site. However, he does have bottle inventory from past vintages.

Cabernet's Greek Ancestor

drawings of Krimbas's 'black volitsa'
(*Elliniki Ampelografia*, Vol. III, p. 87)

βολίτσα μαύρη
volitsa mavri
black volitsa

Desert Island Wine

Miles Lambert-Gócs has been worshipping and pondering Dionysus for decades at his home in Virginia. He turned to creative wine-and-food writing after a career spent penning boiler-plate farm fare for the U.S. Department of Agriculture. His previous book, *Greek Salad: A Dionysian Travelogue* (Wine Appreciation Guild, 2004), is a humorous cellar-and-table-hopping journey through the Wine-god's homeland, greatly enjoyed and praised by aficionados of Greece, ancient or modern. He also authored *The Wines of Greece* (Faber & Faber, 1990), the definitive work on the history and traditions of Greek wine, awarded by the Anglo Hellenic League and The Wine Guild of the United Kingdom, and a finalist for the James Beard Awards. See copyright page for contact information.